AF378661

The *Notes & Queries* Book of People

Paul Howlett and Joseph Harker edit the *Guardian*'s weekly Notes & Queries column.

The *Notes & Queries* Book of People

Edited by
Paul Howlett and Joseph Harker

theguardian

ATLANTIC BOOKS
LONDON

Published in Great Britain in hardback in 2005
by Atlantic Books on behalf of Guardian Newspapers Ltd.
Atlantic Books is an imprint of Grove Atlantic Ltd.

Copyright © Guardian Newspapers Ltd 2005

ISBN 1 84354 455 5

A CIP record for this book is available from the British Library

2 4 6 8 10 9 7 5 3 1

Designed and typeset by Patty Rennie Production, Portsoy
Printed in Great Britain by Mackays of Chatham plc,
Chatham, Kent

Guardian Books
Ormond House
26–27 Boswell Street
London WC1N 3JZ

Contents

Foreword

People. Aren't they amazing? Well, judging by the contributions to the *Guardian*'s ever popular Notes & Queries section they are. In these pages you will find a selection of the funniest and most fascinating questions and answers concerning people in all their glory, all the way from legendary figures such as Alexander the Great, down to the man on the Clapham omnibus.

Like its companion volume – *The Notes & Queries Book of Places* (also available, by the way, at a very reasonable price, in a bookshop near you), we've divided this compilation of the intriguing, the stimulating and the entertaining into handy sections. People at Large covers the big subjects, like life (why is it so hard?), death (has anyone actually died laughing? Or of boredom?) and taxes (what is the most appropriate response to an Inland Revenue demand for 3p?). It also looks at smaller but still vitally important matters: is drinking your own urine good for you? Why doesn't a dishwasher have a window in its door? And do aliens have a moral right to eat us?

Historical People speaks for itself, and will teach you

things you probably won't find in the average history book: why do pirates always have eye-patches and wooden legs? Was the explorer Mungo Park really eaten by zombies? What's the point of string vests? And who first lay back and thought of England? Famous People gives you the lowdown on the lives of household names from Margaret Thatcher to Mother Goose, Richard Wagner to Norbert Dentressangle. And in Fictional People, you can learn where Superman got his muscles, find out whether the ancient Greek physician Asclepius was man or myth, and discover the difference between a Hobbit, an elf, a dwarf and a troll (clue: it seems to have something to do with which newspaper they read, and there's not a *Guardian* type among them).

In People at Play we cover the big sports (What was the worst-ever refereeing decision in a football match? Will 100-metre sprinters go on getting faster and faster, forever? Why do tennis players get two serves?) to higher matters (Why do classical musicians never cough during a concert? What is the longest uninterrupted 'dead' role on stage? Why do opera singers get so fat?) and everyday relaxations (How can you train slugs to eat unwanted garden foliage? Why do we kiss? Why don't women go fishing?).

Finally, People at Work looks at esoteric matters such as the inner workings of secret service departments MI1–MI19; more general issues such as whether milk should go in first or last when pouring tea, and the mysterious disappearance of the French onion men; and, at last, the big question: could there be a more generally fascinating and frivolous job than a Notes & Queries editor? To which the answer – one of very few that won't surprise you in this book – is no.

Paul Howlett and Joseph Harker

PEOPLE AT LARGE

What are the odds against being born?

A woman is born with all her eggs in place. Between the ages of twelve and fifty she will produce roughly 475 viable eggs, if you allow time for a couple of pregnancies. Assuming that she has two children, 473 eggs will go to waste. Someone else will have to work out the odds: all I know is that we are all very lucky to be here.

Gwen Evans, London SW18

The answer is one (that is, a dead certainty). Also, by an appeal to the anthropic principle (which asserts certain facts based on the existence of the observer: the human race), the answer to 'What are the chances of the universe coming in to being?' is also one. Douglas Adams came up with forty-two, for reasons that escape me.

Gordon Joly, London E14

If you mean, 'What are the odds against your being born as the unique individual you obviously are', then the odds are as close to 100 per cent as you can get and it's an absolute miracle. First, you had to make it safely into this world, your mother had to be born and survive long enough to give birth to you, and your father had to survive and meet your mother. Their parents had to do so as well. And their parents, and theirs back through time. Just think of the infinite number of things that might have gone wrong along the way. Childbirth was tricky thousands of years ago, and the chances of two people meeting at all depend on an infinity of coincidences. Any break in this chain would mean you would be someone else.

On the other hand: if you are reading this while drinking your morning coffee, then the odds must be 100 per cent that it all happened just like that, and zero that it didn't.

Christiane Hare, Rooksbridge, Somerset

The odds are heavily against being born. Aldous Huxley expressed them in round figures in his poem, 'Fifth Philosopher's Song': 'A million million spermatozoa,/All of them alive:/Out of their cataclysm but one poor Noah/Dare hope to survive.'

Les Gorse, Morecambe, Lancs

Buddha described the odds against being born human (as opposed to being born as an animal, hell-being, hungry spirit or god) with an analogy. Imagine there is a blind turtle living at the bottom of a vast and deep ocean the size of the world, and on the surface of the ocean floats a golden yoke. Once in every hundred years, the turtle surfaces. The odds against the turtle raising its head through the middle of the yoke are the same as being born human.

Sam Bain, London SW16

The odds against being born? Nothing like as good as those against dying.

David Cottis, London SE1

Do love potions exist?

Yes. All you need is seventy-seven leaves of lovage picked at dawn after a night of full moon (mind you only pick the leaves that have dew on them), 100 ml of Polish bison grass vodka, a copper cauldron and a crystal vodka glass. Put the vodka bottle in the fridge. Stew the leaves all day with a little water (rainwater is best), adding a few tears for flavour. Strain the leaves through a fine-mesh sieve and set aside the green liquid to cool. Half an hour before your beloved is due, put the crystal glass (empty) in the freezer. Pour the green liquid down the sink, and the vodka into the chilled glass (it should smoke) and give it him to drink.

Works every time.

Ania Plank, Chesham Bois, Bucks

They exist all right, no doubt about it. I think the question you want to ask is: do they work? I have no hard evidence, but the known effects of other herbal medicines suggest that it should be feasible to produce a mixture of herbs that could produce elevated levels of phenyethylamine and associated neurotransmitters in the brain. This would increase the probability of igniting the flames of romantic love in those sharing the drink. However, the case history of Tristan and Yseult suggests that love potions should only be administered by a fully qualified medical practitioner in a controlled setting.

Richard Lawson, Congresbury, Somerset

Yes. Yes. Yes. Yes; yes; yes; yes, yes, yes, yyyyyeeeeesssssss.

Geoff Reiss, Wetherby, Yorks

If person A is unrequitedly in love with person B, does person B have any moral obligation or duties towards A?

The notion that one can 'fall in love' with someone who

does not reciprocate the feeling is a latter-day fallacy. Love has very little to do with erotic attraction, and nothing at all to do with the often urgent need to pacify one's own feelings of loneliness or insufficiency.

Sounds to me like person A is projecting a supposed solution to their own neurosis on to person B. Person B has a duty I hope we all recognize – to look after others and ourselves, and to use the force of our personalities in a productive and compassionate way.

Failing the above, dysfunctional relationships of dependency may be curtailed by the use of extreme physical violence.

Simon Phillips, London W9

A similar problem was considered by Spinoza in the seventeenth century in his *Ethics*. Spinoza came to the conclusion that a man who loves God cannot expect God to love him in return. In the following century the great German poet and thinker Goethe advanced the argument and succinctly wrote: 'I love you, why should that be any concern of yours!'

If an attempt is made at a definition of love, perhaps one of the best that we can come up with is: unconditional positive regard. If this definition is accepted, then it is easily seen that the notion of B having any obligations or duties towards A involves a contradiction in terms.

Kant considered that feelings of affection could not be

demanded of us as a duty. Kant also believed strongly in the autonomy of human personality. I am sure that he would also support the view that the question must be answered in the negative.

Douglas N. Passant, London E4

Love, in effect, is an emotional contract between two people. Person B would have no moral obligation – unless, by word or deed, he/she accepted the contract.

Simon Vogel, Harlow, Essex

A recent television programme stated that men between the ages of thirty-five and fifty-five were the grumpiest creatures on the planet. So what do we have to look forward to that will mysteriously cheer us all up when we hit fifty-six?

Bugger all.

Nick Gregory (Aged 56½), Ashton-under-Lyne, Lancs

Premature senility.

Geoff Booth, Knebworth, Herts

The realisation that it will all be over soon.

Nick Foreman, Chorleywood, Herts

Has anyone actually died laughing?

Forgive the paraphrasing and extracting of chunks of text, but in *The Book of Lists 2* (Corgi, 1981) there is a section devoted to deaths where excessive laughter appeared to be at least the primary cause. These included Zeuxis, a fifth-century BC Greek painter who laughed so hard at a painting he'd done of an old woman, he choked to death; the Greek poet Philemon who died in 263 BC laughing at one of his own jests; and Chrysippus, a Greek (are we seeing a pattern here?) philosopher in the third century BC who died laughing at the sight of a donkey eating figs (I guess one had to be there).

Then there was Pietro Aretino, an Italian author (1492–1556) who, laughing at a bawdy story, fell backwards and died; and Mrs Fitzherbert, an English widow who laughed so hard at a production of *The Beggar's Opera* in 1782 that she eventually expired the next day, still laughing.

Finally, Alex Mitchell (1925–75), a bricklayer of King's Lynn, laughed so hard at the TV show *The Goodies* (the episode featuring 'Ecky Thump') that he succumbed to a heart attack. Allegedly, his widow bore no grudge and wrote to The Goodies thanking them for making her husband's last moments so happy.

David Newell, Leeds

My grandma, Elsie Robinson, died in 1953 from a heart attack while laughing in the cinema during a showing of *Doctor in the House*. Sadly there wasn't one.

Graham Robinson, Hexham, Northumberland

My grandfather Edwin and his friend Ernest sat on a park bench watching bowling. Ernest told Edwin a joke and nudged him in the ribs. My grandfather laughed so much he fell off the bench, dead. The death certificate suggested he died from a heart attack. I like to think he died laughing.

Helen Hackett, Durham

Sir Thomas Urquhart (1611–60), a royalist exiled abroad, is reputed to have died laughing on hearing that Charles II had been restored.

David Craig, Bromsgrove, Worcs

What was the joke that Helen Hackett's grandfather's friend told that caused her grandfather to die?

Sheila Coe, Skipton, North Yorks

Sheila Coe asks that we be told the joke that caused Helen Hackett's grandfather to die laughing. Has she considered the potentially fatal consequences? Does she harbour a deep antipathy towards N&Q readers?

Pam Laurance, London NW10

With regard to the joke that killed my grandfather – if such a weapon of comedic mass destruction were to fall into the wrong hands, I fear the consequences would be catastrophic.

Helen Hackett, Durham

The idea of a hypothetical joke that would make people who hear it die laughing was actually in one of *Monty Python*'s earliest sketches, the irony being that it is one of their less funny inventions and is certainly not going to make anybody die laughing. The joke in question gets deployed against the Germans in the Second World War as, yes, a weapon of mass destruction (although that phrase was not known when the sketch was written, of course).

Frank Desmond, London SE7

John Kipling did. One of Rudyard's 'Epitaphs of the War' goes: 'My son was killed while laughing at some jest. I would I knew/What it was, and it might serve me in a time when jests are few.'

John Jacobs, Lewes, East Sussex

I have just received from the Inland Revenue – by first-class post and enclosing a first-class-post prepaid envelope – a demand for underpaid tax of 3p. What is the most appropriate response?

I once received a demand for unpaid tax of £0.00p that was followed by a series of further demands and then threats of court action if I didn't pay up. They stopped only when I sent them a cheque for the amount. It never appeared on my bank statement.

John Ratcliffe, Ripon, North Yorks

Why is there such a fine line between pleasure and pain?

Because we are greedy, and we are subject to habituation. This means that we get accustomed to a stimulus to our senses, so the chocolate pie that once tasted so delicious, the horror of that startling film, the thrill of a dangerous sport, the sensual pleasure from whatever once excited us: we no longer derive quite the same joy from these as we did the first time around. We crave ever more intense sensory inputs to maintain the same level of 'happiness', as measured by levels of brain chemicals that are produced when in a satisfied state of mind.

Unfortunately, as the human brain seeks more extreme stimulation, the human body has a job to do, to maintain a fairly constant internal environment within quite narrow limits of temperature, levels of oxygen, carbon dioxide, fats, sugars etc. But many pleasurable stimulations also physically affect the body, and we are inevitably going to come into conflict between the aims of increasing brain excitement and avoiding internal bodily disruption. The latter causes pain signals to the brain as a warning: 'Stop this or your life-support systems will be compromised.'

If this sounds like a recipe for the fading of all pleasures in older age, keep your pleasure sources varied. That will prevent habituation, keep you joyful and maybe extend your lifespan.

(Dr) Hillary Shaw, Southampton

It is a truism that many of life's opposites have a point on the spectrum where they become indistinguishable – pleasure and pain, hot and cold, even fascism and communism.

Happiness, beyond a certain point, can slip into the realms of the poignant and bittersweet.

This is the universe acting as counterbalance, for fear we slide too far in one direction. Its message: moderation in all things.

Titus Anatschev, Dunstable, Beds

The answer has been known for thousands of years: 'contraria sunt complementa' (opposites are complementary).

Douglas Jaggers, Derby

My boyfriend would like to give me a diamond, but the idea of wearing something that reflects the pain suffered by underpaid miners in countries torn by civil war is repulsive. Does a politically correct diamond exist?

I've thought of a way for you to maintain your moral stance: get your boyfriend to buy the ring and give it to me! Problem solved.

Monique Darrell, London WC1

Why do women in lonely hearts ads invariably ask for men with a sense of humour?

Conflicting definitions of humour account for this. When women say 'sense of humour', we don't mean the 'have you heard the one about' variety. We mean an ability to respond creatively and supportively to whoever has been talking.

To test this theory, watch any single-sex group in a pub: in the women's group all are talking and laughing; in the men's group one talks, the others laugh (or don't, depending on his status or the punchline). So when women ask for a sense of humour, they are simply looking for a partner who can listen.

Tessa Tointon, London EC1

Call me cynical if you will, but I always assumed it meant
Good Salary, Own House (or in the shires, Horse).

Terry Adams, Birmingham

Because they're looking for someone special.

Justin Dillon, London SE1

**Over the past 2,500 years, some of the best brains
that humankind has produced have studied the
problems of philosophy. What problems of
relevance to everyday life have they solved?**

Before the nineteenth century, there was no science
and there were no scientists, and what we would now
call science was done by philosophers. Democritus con-
tributed the atomic theory of matter; Archimedes his
screw (still used in jacks and pumps as well as to propel
ships and aircraft); Pascal the theory of probability;
Copernicus modern astronomy; Newton the dynamics
that are still universally useful in engineering; Hobbes
artificial intelligence (thinking as calculation); and so
on.

Today, when we don't know how to set about solving
a problem (when there is no established scientific method),
we have to step back a pace and do philosophy – we have
to think about the way we think until we can come up

with a new scientific method or even a completely new science. Then we can get back to work and stop philosophising until we get stuck again. Indeed, anybody who finds himself in difficulties in work or life and stops to think about the way he is working or living, instead of pressing on in the old way, is doing philosophy.

Grahame Leman, London W3

Philosophers are sometimes criticized for arguing among themselves, but artists and scientists argue among themselves too. Artists have brought you costume drama, scientists have brought you television, but philosophers have brought you the right to vote; the right not to be sold into slavery; the right to trial by jury and equality before the law; freedom of speech . . . Sufficiently relevant to everyday life?

Michael Hampson, Harlow, Essex

The questioner should ask, first of all, if he/she would even be able to pose the question without the study of philosophy.

Edward Carter, Department of Artificial Intelligence,
University of Edinburgh

Philosophers do not solve problems, but create them in forms ever more difficult to solve, thus perpetuating philosophy. This is not unique: economists, sociologists and politicians behave in exactly the same way with corresponding consequences.

(Prof.) Sir James Beament, Queens' College, Cambridge

At the last lecture of my moral philosophy course our professor said: 'Don't think you're no further forward. The value of studying philosophy is that you've reached a more informed state of ignorance.'

Alan Brown, Glasgow

If God were actually to exist, would he be concerned if we believed in him/her or not?

One place to look for an answer is Neale Donald Walsch's *Conversations With God* series. Mind-blowing stuff. 'God' has no preference about belief, or anything else. We just think he/she/it does. Of the many illusions we live by, that's the most powerful of all, so powerful that millions have fought – and continue to fight – over it.

But you don't have to believe in God, or in Walsch's conversations, to acknowledge this. Ultimately, the best place to find the answers is not in books – or indeed the pages of the *Guardian* – but within. So long as you believe in a self that is separate (another powerful illusion) or a God that is 'out there looking down' and 'needing something' from us, e.g. belief, you've missed the point – the truth of who you really are. 'I and the Father are one,' as someone once said.

So, deep down, paradoxically, you already are 'that which you seek'; and you actually know the answer to this question – even before you've asked it.

Steve Turnbull, Huddersfield

To ask such a question is to 'humanize' God/the divine. God, or whatever name we choose to give the highest universal source, loves all creation unconditionally, and so I would suggest that the answer is 'no'.

While we are on the earthly plane, we have free will entirely, although we might have particular life themes to experience when here. Many believe (and this includes me) that we are eternal, and elect to undergo a number of incarnations on earth. Perhaps part of one's life theme or spiritual path might be to question the existence of a higher force, and then maybe, or maybe not, rediscover the divine within, before going home to the spiritual realms.

As we currently experience a huge shift in consciousness (the age of Pisces is almost at a close), many people are questioning long-held beliefs about God. This is part of our earthly and spiritual evolution, and yes, it's absolutely fine to question everything.

Ian Henderson, Wigan, Lancs

God would clearly not need our belief, but he/she would surely not wish us to live in ignorance.

Michael Henesy, Edinburgh

Why do sandwiches taste better when sliced diagonally?

For the same reason that diagonally sliced toast does.

Pete Whittle, Canterbury

It's because you get a longer surface of crustless bread with the filling showing where one bites into the sandwich. The length of the side opposite the right-angled triangle is longer than the side of the square. A small sandwich, either square or triangular, with all the crusts cut off, tastes the same! My mathematically minded partner has been writing down all kinds of formulae but I think it is obvious if you draw a square and halve it down the middle then across from one corner to another and measure the lines.

Mary Ann Reed, London N10

The question is based on a contestable assertion. My mother was at a loss as to how to satisfy her family of hungry boys on this matter. We knew that sandwiches should be cut horizontally, but competed fiercely for the ends that were square rather than rounded. I can't help thinking that this recurrent family squabble of more than forty years ago found its way into the market-research zeitgeist, resulting in all the square loaves available today.

The corners, which we apparently prized so highly, consisted of crust, and these were carefully hidden under the rims of our plates, a practice that I assume is ubiquitous among small boys. On reflection, our actions must always have been revealed in our absence when Mum cleared the table, yet still we persisted. I wonder what else we thought we had got away with, when the only real phenomenon at work was Mum's patience.

Jeff Lewis, Exmouth

Is it true that women can do more things at the same time than men?

No, it's just that we're expected to.

Marie Marshall, Dundee

I can't answer that question AND type at the same time.

Luke Cumiskey, Molesey, Surrey

Is it possible to remember being born?

My experience, as a provider and user of alternative healing therapies, suggests that most people retain this memory, although at a subconscious level. I know of many people who have remembered or re-experienced their birth, either through hypnosis, the use of consciousness-expanding drugs, or rebirthing therapy. The latter employs guided meditation in combination with breathing exercises.

In our culture most of us experience birth as a traumatic event. The most common problem is when the placenta is cut too soon, before the infant has cleared his lungs of liquid and has begun to breathe air normally. When this happens, the new soul experiences a sensation of suffocation. This leaves a stark emotional imprint on the new baby: 'This world is harsh, and life-threatening; and so I must be fearful.' It is far better to gently place the infant on the mother's stomach, and wait patiently until the baby is breathing regularly. Then the placenta can be severed without trauma.

A change in our birthing procedures would have a most profound beneficial effect on the psychological health and wellbeing of our future citizens.

> *Geoffrey Sigworth, The Centre for Holistic Wellness,*
> *Johnstown, Pennsylvania, US*

Masked and distorted birth memories are a prime suspect in the cases of alien abduction experiences: there is the initial paralysis; frequent feelings of weightlessness; terror; a bright light (frequently blinding) and ultimately an examination by unfamiliar humanoids (who are nearly always embryo-like, with large heads, spindly limbs, undefined faces and memorable eyes). Finally, there is a feeling of epiphany or heightened consciousness, and (in most cases) a profound, self-sealing amnesia.

If nothing else, this possibility would explain why the aliens seem so preoccupied with fertility and sex: they are from inner space, not outer.

Garrick Alder, London SW2

Would humankind have evolved differently if the dinosaurs had not disappeared 65 million years ago?

If the dinosaurs had not disappeared, humankind simply wouldn't exist. At their height, the dinosaurs had a firm clawhold on just about every animal niche, from three-feet-tall egg-stealers up to 45-ton herbivores. When the dinosaurs became extinct, the mammal line consisted essentially of scruffy little beasts that danced around their toes and tried not to get trodden on. It was only terrible luck that consigned the lizards to the evolutionary dustbin and let the versatile, but frankly pathetic, mammals enter the arena and flourish. Whatever it was that caused the demise of the dinosaurs, it must also have been enough to ensure that the peanut-brained placentals would eventually become intelligent primates. The potential for intellectual development had never solely been ours.

Duncan McMillan, London N6

There would be car stickers with the message: 'A stegosaurus is for life, not just for Christmas.'

Graham Guest, London SE19

The intervening years would have given ample time for adaptive strategies to compensate for our giant reptile companions. Many of us would probably have evolved to be inedible (perhaps covered with poisonous sacs), or to stick in hungry dino throats (resembling large walking chestnut burrs with access to language).

Reuben Saunders, New York, US

Yes, we'd be able to run much faster.

Jeff Williams, Hengoed, Mid Glamorgan

Is it true that there are more people alive today than dead?

Not even close. It is estimated that in 50,000 years of human history, more than 100 billion (in the American sense of billion as a thousand million) human beings have been born. Most estimates run somewhat higher. There are fewer than 6.4 billion alive today. There are, then, about 15 dead, probably more, for every living person on earth.

The story about more alive than dead began to circulate rather widely back in the late sixties or early seventies, but I have never been able to locate a source. Does anyone know?

William Dunlap, Hamden, Connecticut, US

If all the people in the world lined up in the first rank of a rectangle of people, and all their ancestors going back to the first human from 5 million years ago filled in the ranks behind them, then the rectangle would be 6 billion long but only fifteen deep.

Hazel Ruxton, Glasgow

The fifteen-deep theory only accounts for those lines of descent that manifest themselves now. What about the countless lines that have died out over the ages, which are now unrepresented by those living today?

Martin Palmer, Manchester

Huge quantities of human hair are thrown away by hairdressing salons. Could they be used?

A couple of years ago, a friend of mine, realizing that chemo would leave her without hair, had her waist-length locks carefully cut off, plaited and shipped to an organisation that makes wigs for children undergoing chemo — a nice bit of recycling, I would say; and, though my friend is gone, she lives on, on several young heads around the country.

Gil Shorr, Los Angeles, US

Why are women generally smaller than men?

Men have generally been taller than women since Neolithic times. However, the difference in height has been reducing over the years and, from research I carried out some years ago, it seems that the difference in height between the sexes is now less pronounced. Even so, it is not likely that women and men will eventually be the same average height. Much of the growth in our long bones occurs before puberty. Hormonal changes at puberty slow down the rate of growth, and because females reach puberty at an earlier age than males, they have a shorter time in which their long bones can grow.

Graham Jones, Thatcham, Newbury, Berks

It's because God, like the Japanese, improved on his

earlier model by making a more compact and sophisticated design.

Dinah Pollock, Huyton, Merseyside

Dinah Pollock is wrong about men being the earlier model. For a few million years, life was female and self-producing only. We only invented men because we were getting bored.

Mary-Rose Benton, Stourport-on-Severn, Worcs

Has anyone ever died of boredom?

Dean W. R. Inge was accurate in his contention (see *The End of an Age*, 1948) that: 'The effect of boredom on a large scale in history is underestimated. It is a main cause of revolutions.' The answer has to be yes, lots.

(The Rev.) Clifford Warren, Machen Rectory, Gwent

Boredom has certainly been responsible for a number of deaths, often by mistake. Louis XIV regularly started wars out of sheer boredom. In Chicago in 1924, Nathan Leopold and Michael Loeb plotted the murder of a schoolboy, just as a relief for their interminable ennui. Death has also been caused in trivial moments of tedium: on 3 November 1973, a passenger was killed on a DC10 because an engine exploded after a bored flight engineer had meddled with a few of the buttons in the cockpit.

Although Samuel Beckett's two tramps in *Waiting For Godot* might be suffering a terminal boredom when they whine 'we are bored to death', and Nasa is worried that it may well cause serious problems on a manned mission to Mars, it's unlikely that boredom leads to the final decision to die rather than continue a life of bland indifference. In the words of Morrissey, that guru of bedsit boredom: 'I think about life and I think about death/And neither one particularly appeals to me.'

John Dutton and Chris Horrocks,
London N4

On 31 July 1861, whichever of the Goncourt brothers was on journal duty that day asked whether their lack of success might actually mean they were failures. He then adds: 'One thing reassures me as to our value: the boredom that afflicts us. It is the hallmark of quality in modern men. Chateaubriand died of it, long before his death. Byron was stillborn with it.'

Richard Boston, Reading, Berks

Why is the most common form of heterosexual coupling called the missionary position?

Isn't the missionary position the one recommended by lay preachers?

Philip Oliver, Burton upon Trent, Staffs

This appears to be so-called not because it was used by missionaries (although that was probably the case) but because it was the position missionaries are supposed to have advocated for the 'lesser races' they were preaching to. There seem to be two reasons for this preference. The face-to-face position was thought more 'civilized' than other 'animalistic' ones and, second, it literally put the man on top. In this way the position embodied two key aspects of the nineteenth-century middle-class view of the world.

The evidence of sex positions in the past suggests that it was by no means the most preferred and perhaps not the most common. Presumably the missionaries encountered a situation where it was not so common; otherwise they would not have had to advocate it. The rise of the missionary position, therefore, seems to be related to the intensification of a male-dominated, imperialist, class society. But contemporary sex surveys also suggest that men and women often get more pleasure from alternative positions. Readers sympathetic towards the Labour party's current abandonment of class politics might like to consider the significance this has for their own lives. Not only are revolutionary positions more politically correct, they are also likely to be more fun.

Mike Haynes, Telford Socialist Workers Party, Telford, Shrops

I am fairly certain that Mike Haynes of the Socialist Workers Party has, unsurprisingly, adopted the wrong position over missionaries. The missionary position was not advocated by them but was their conventional mode and observed as such by inquisitive islanders in the depth of the Polynesian night. One matter is, however, illuminated by Haynes: the reluctance of SWP members to look one another in the eye.

R. A. Leeson, Broxbourne, Herts

If the devil is trying to recruit people to evil, why doesn't he make hell a more attractive final destination?

The devil does not need to recruit people to evil: we are that way inclined already. That is why Jesus said: 'No one can see the kingdom of God [in heaven] unless he is born again.' If we are content to go to hell, we don't need to actively do anything, merely continue in the way we were conceived. That said, the devil has given hell the greatest promotion of all time: ask almost anyone in the street and they will tell you that hell doesn't exist. For the place where the devil and all who follow him are going to be punished day and night for ever, I don't think anyone could really do better than that!

Peter Middleton, Newport, Gwent

Heard in Switzerland: A sanctimonious politician dies, is welcomed to heaven by God and shown the refrigerator in case he feels like a snack. Peering over the lip of a cloud he spies, down in hell, a mouth-watering banquet in full swing. Why, he demands, are there only pots of yoghurt in the celestial fridge? God shrugs: 'No point in cooking just for the two of us, is there?'

Kathryn Smits, Auckland, New Zealand

I bumped into a friend the other day but had forgotten his name. I know that he had forgotten mine too. How do you get out of such an embarrassing situation?

It's just as bad when you do remember the name. A few years ago I met a woman called Claire I'd known for a month or two a few years previously. We both greeted each other by name, but after a few minutes, it became clear that she was a different Claire who looked a little like mine, and I was a different Nik who looked a little like hers. When I subsequently met the real Claire at a party a couple of months later, she thought I was someone completely different for a good half hour, while I called her Cathy and asked after her long-dead boyfriend.

Nik Devlin, London SW9

Urine is said to be sterile. Can this be so when it is bodily waste? And is there any truth in the Indian belief that drinking one's own urine is good for you?

If you are going to drink your own urine, should you wash your hands before or afterwards?

Derek Seddon, Cheadle, Cheshire

Urine in the bladder is sterile, unless there is a urinary tract infection or possibly a renal infection. The odour comes from nitrogenous wastes – the end products of protein metabolism – and uric acid. Nitrogen-containing compounds have the typical acrid aroma because of single- or double-bonded nitrogen atoms, depending on the compound. There may also be metabolites of medications a person is taking or the methyl mercaptan excreted after eating asparagus, for example.

As the urine passes through the end of the urethra, it may pick up some normal skin flora, but this will be washed away with the flow of urine.

Drinking urine would be beneficial in one instance: if

there were absolutely no other fluids of any kind available. A pair of functioning kidneys are very effective at getting rid of what we don't need, so why treat them as if they were cowboy builders who needed to re-do the job?

Marybeth Swiger, Vancouver, Canada

I have been drinking my own urine on a daily basis for about five years with no ill effects and have found it to be a good remedy for dehydration, among other things. I also practise the yoga technique of *neti*, cleansing the nostrils using my own urine (it is recommended that if you follow these practices you keep to a vegetarian diet).

Liz Gray, Leicester

Exactly this question was asked in N&Q on 7 January 1988. My answer, which you published then, has not changed. I still do not recommend it. It will no doubt still taste like piss, the only part of my answer you omitted to print.

Philip Brett, Yelverton, Devon

Is megalomania a treatable condition?

Never! Never! Ha, ha, ha, ha, ha . . . !

William Merrin, Wakefield.

It is fully curable. I went for treatment at a small clinic outside Paris and was so impressed with its methods that I took over the running of it, and this is only the beginning . . .

David May, London SW20

Do people who work live longer than people who live a life of leisure? In other words, if I retire at fifty and go to live in Spain, is my life expectancy more or less than the people I've left behind at the office?

When I was in my mid-fifties and thinking of retiring early, I was advised by a personnel director that people who retired aged fifty-five lived for another twenty-five years, and that people who retired aged sixty-five only lived for another five years. I don't know whether this is true, but it made my mind up to go early – and it was certainly my best career move.

Jack Jones, Plymouth

In the case of NHS consultants at least, there is evidence that early retirement increases life expectancy. A study carried out about fifteen years ago showed that practitioners who retired at sixty lived an average two to three years longer than colleagues working until sixty-five. Partly on the strength of this report I retired at sixty and having reached my seventy-fifth year in good health, have no reason to regret the decision.

Bob Heys, Halifax

Much of my work as a reflexologist has been to help clients reach an understanding of how lifestyle factors – such as their job – can have a profound effect on their general health and susceptibility to disease.

This was clearly explained by the pioneering endocrinologist Hans Selye in his book *The Stress of Life* (1956). He distinguished between good kinds of stress that cause us to grow and develop, and negative stresses that wear us down. When we perceive a situation to be threatening in some way, or suffer an emotional loss or simply have too much to do, the body mounts what is termed a 'stress response', a complex sequence of nervous and hormonal activity. If this response occurs very frequently, not allowing the body to recuperate and normalize, there are significantly deleterious implications for our health.

We often find by changing our attitude, and therefore our response to stresses, they cease to affect us in this way. But speaking for myself, I'll see you in Spain.

Emma Brooker, Bath

According to George Bernard Shaw, 'A perpetual holiday is a good working definition of hell.'

Keith Hopper, Oxford

When my young children asked where they were before they were in mummy's tummy, I could only come up with 'nowhere'. Does anyone have a more satisfactory answer?

They weren't anywhere. They were preconceptions.

Gordon Jackson, Hyde, Cheshire

Half of you was inside mummy, half of you was inside daddy, then we joined those halves together and made the whole you.

Nicci Salmon, London SW6

You are contemplating the wonder of the creation of your children out of nothing; there was no 'before'. Whether you choose scientific language or religious language to express it, stand in awe of it.

(The Rev.) Michael Hampson, Harlow, Essex

The questioner should introduce his children to gardening. Even young children can grasp the concept that plants produce seeds which, given the right conditions, can grow into plants. Children can then be told that they began life as a seed that 'mummy' produced inside her 'tummy' just as a plant produces seeds. They can then be told that they did not exist before the seed was produced, the same way as a plant did not 'exist' before the seed was produced.

Later, the questioner could explain that the 'seeds' that mummy produces are called eggs, which are just like birds' eggs, but instead of hatching in a nest, they grow inside mummy. When the children start asking about egg fertilization, they are ready for the full unexpurgated explanation: for this, I am sure the local library will have a wide range of helpful books.

Angus Baxter, West Lothian, Scotland

If the next sperm in the queue had fertilized my mother's egg, would I have been in various ways different or would someone else have been conceived in my place?

The idea that I would still exist even if my mother had married a different father, or if conception had taken place a month later than it actually did, or if the second spermatozoon had won the race to the ovum, originates with St Thomas Aquinas, who held that the soul is infused into the body at the moment of conception. Presumably my soul was positioned, somewhere, to join with the newly formed embryo as soon as the egg was fertilized. If fertilization was delayed, so was I.

If we disregard the notion of 'soul' and look at what happens when a fertilized egg splits to form identical twins, we realize that we get two discrete human identities where before there was only one. The same is true when the connection is cut between the two upper hemispheres of the brain: two separate spheres of consciousness are created, i.e. two different identities in one body.

Clearly, a particular human identity originates with a particular functioning human brain, and we must therefore deduce that if the next sperm in the queue had fertilized my mother's egg, I would not exist. That means my existence depended on 'my' spermatozoon arriving at 'my' ovum before the 3 billion or so other spermatozoa who were having a go.

(Dr) Andre Blom, Waterloo, Ontario, Canada

What is the evolutionary advantage to teenagers being inconsiderate, uncooperative, lazy, untidy and rude? Or are these characteristics seen only in modern Western culture and not among hunter-gatherers?

I think it is a product of affluent Western society coupled with hormonal imbalance. In the developing world people spend much more energy on staying alive, rather than feeling so much depressing, destructive, social pressure from their peers. It may be relevant to say that hunter-gatherers didn't live too long anyway, and never had the chance to experience much of an adolescence.

Depending on the period, some were lucky to make it to fifteen.

Ian Sutty, Nottingham

This transition stage is also observed in monkeys. Males tend to fight each other more, while the females tend to be slightly more boisterous. The fact is that teenage years are important in the development of identity. We find our place in the world, and what we want to do with the rest of our life. By being 'inconsiderate, uncooperative, lazy and rude', as you so eloquently put it, we become our own person, do we not? You seem a very rude and inconsiderate person yourself. Are you a teenager? Thought not.

Rebecca Erin Connolly, aged 18, Glasgow

I tend to think that being a rude, lazy, etc. teenager depends on which society you live in. As a matter of fact, hunter-gatherer societies avoided this problem by shifting directly from childhood to adulthood, through various ceremonies (i.e. becoming a man on a particular ceremonial day). But history doesn't tell whether these new men were behaving as such, or being lazy, rude, etc.

Laetitia Favre, Evian-les-Bains, France

It's nature's way of making parents glad to see the back of them.

Jake Arnott, Bristol

That question is SO TYPICAL!

Andrew Taylor, Cambridge

Do you eat soup or drink it?

Doesn't it depend on the consistency of the soup – how lumpy it is, or how many bits it has in it?

Katherine Ellis, London

Surely it depends whether you're using a spoon or not? If you use a spoon you're eating, if you slurped it out of the bowl (or indeed mug) then you are drinking it.

Jill Weekley, Reading

Probably both. If you chew the soup, you are eating it. If you swallow it without chewing, you are drinking it (or about to choke).

Stephen Grasser, Salluit, Canada

Why does wearing a hat impair one's driving ability?

Ask Michael Schumacher.

Donald Hind, Harwich, Essex

We need to differentiate between different headgear. A reversed baseball cap is bad, but is not generally in sight long enough to seriously affect you. Anyway, the pounding bass stereo gives sufficient warning to take evasive action. Far worse, and much more persistent, is the flat cap, especially if worn by the elderly male driver of a Volvo estate. The impairment is compounded tenfold if that driver is towing a caravan on the M5 near Exeter.

Richard Fryer, Sutton Coldfield, West Mids

I must confess to often wearing a flat cap when I'm driving and I can only say that this seems to bring out the protective instinct of the helpless brigade. Quite often I find one of these drivers snuggling up to my rear bumper – even at 60 mph. Obviously their radar has picked up that I'm nearing seventy years and they want to be on the spot to assist if I should pass out. Their concern is very touching, but I mustn't be selfish. He/she may be on an urgent errand of mercy, so if I feel I will last another five minutes, I will try to let them pass.

When, eventually and reluctantly, they decide to overtake, they will try to lovingly caress the front corner of my car. And a mile down the road, they will be showing the same concern to another driver.

Hatless drivers – I take my hat off to you!

P. Koenig, Headcorn, Kent

I think Richard Fryer's answer is silly. I have been driving an open Bentley for over forty years and a flat cap is essential. It keeps the rain off one's hair and the sun out of one's eyes, and so improves my driving ability.

Brian Bentley, Hay-on-Wye, Hereford

I have been told that a male child will always grow up to be taller than his mother. Is this true?

Predicting a child's adult height depends on both the mother's and the father's height. It is calculated by adding 12.5 cm to the mother's height and then taking the average of this figure and the father's height. The child's adult height should then fall within +/− 8.5 cm of this predicted value. According to this formula if the father is no more than 4.5 cm taller than the mother, then it would be possible for the son to be shorter than the mother.

(Dr) Robert Boon, London SE5

If humans were grown to be eaten by a race of aliens, where would the best cuts of meat be found?

Why do you want to know?

Frank Readhead, Cambridge

If aliens were considering eating us they would need to have a comparable carbon-based physiology to ours. For the silicon-based creatures dreamed up by some sci-fi writers, to eat us would be like us eating sand. These carbon aliens would also need either similar protein-based bodies to ours or a very efficient digestion system that could break down the molecules in their food to very simple constituents, for example water, carbon dioxide, ammonia, methane, hydrogen sulphide and sulphur dioxide (I wouldn't want to be around when they burp). Otherwise, them eating us would be like us trying to eat crude oil, say.

Given this, they would likely prefer the protein-based easily digestible bits like the thigh muscles; avoiding less digestible bits like bone, tendons and cartilage (gristle). They might consider at least some of our internal organs a delicacy. A bit like our preferences for which bits of cow, pig, sheep, etc. to eat.

(Dr) Hillary Shaw, Leeds

If we were visited by aliens from an advanced civilization, would we accept that they had a moral right to eat us, hunt us and test new drugs on us, given their higher intelligence?

We would be wrong to assume that moral superiority

accompanies higher intelligence. If this were so, there would be no need for a Serious Fraud Office.

And if the aliens were, in fact, moral beings, they would accept that it is wrong to cause undue pain and distress to other beings. What differentiates us from other animals is that we are not only sentient but self-conscious, with an imagination that would enable us to be aware of what the aliens had in store for us. However kindly we were treated, we would know (as other animals do not) that, sooner or later, we would be hunted or be the subject of experiments or killed and eaten. That would cause continuous and inescapable terror. That would be immoral.

Malcolm Hurwitt, Southall, Middx

We could never accept that they had a moral right to eat us, but they might.

Dick Pountain, London NW1

We are already being visited by aliens and probably have been for millions of years, if the suggestion that viruses emanate from space is true. They attack and consume us — and who is to say that they do not have the moral right to do so if it ensures their continuing existence? Maybe, like Hoyle's Black Cloud hovering in space, they have a far greater 'intelligence' than ours, which enables them to scour the universe for hosts.

Brian Palmer, St Albans, Herts

The leader of the British military mission to Russia in 1939 was Admiral Sir Reginald Plunkett-Ernle-Erle-Drax. Is this the longest hyphenated surname in the UK, and how does a person aspire to have such a surname?

The name of the explorer, Sir Ranulph Twisleton-Wykeham-Fiennes, contains more letters (thirty-three) than that queried (thirty-two), but with only three barrels to Sir Reginald's four. As to how the name was acquired, many complex names (not necessarily hyphenated) are the result of marriages, alliances and so forth. The Fiennes family was given the name Wykeham in the Civil War, as a reward for preventing the desecration by the Round-heads of William of Wykeham's tomb in Winchester cathedral.

Arabella McIntyre Brown, Liverpool

Our formal family name just beats Plunkett-Ernle-Erle-Drax (twenty-one letters) viz: Hovell-Thurlow-Cumming-Bruce (twenty-five letters). Needless to say, we all abbreviate it. When I was up at Trinity College, Cambridge, it was a curiosity much appreciated by tourists passing the hall doors at the foot of the staircase to my rooms to see the whole rigmarole, prefaced 'Hon AP', painted upon the lintel, and followed by 'The Earl Kitchener' and 'The Earl Jellicoe'. There's class! This dotty accumulation derived from the eighteenth and nineteenth-century usage of a husband's hyphenating his wife's name if she was heiress to landed property. In our case H-T also then elected to marry C-B.

Alec Cumming Bruce, Durham

In the event that you do not receive a suitable explanation from a member of the Drax family, perhaps the chauffeur's daughter can outline the cause of all the hyphens. The admiral's ancestors were far better at breeding daughters than sons, so that when Miss Plunkett (a relative of Lord Dunsany, the eminent author) married Mr Ernle, their daughter was Miss Plunkett-Ernle. She married Mr Erle; their daughter, Miss Plunkett-Ernle-Erle, married Mr Drax and Reginald got all the surnames. After four or five daughters, Reginald begot a son, who is known as plain Mr Drax. He has dismally failed to maintain the family tradition and has four or five sons. His eldest son is married to the Princess Royal's former lady-in-waiting, Zara (yes, that's where the name came from) Something-Something. If she threw in her maiden name, her children would be Something-Something-Plunkett-Ernle-Erle-Drax. Of more value than the admiral's abortive mission to Stalin was his pioneering interest in solar heating (for his swimming pool).

(Ms) V. E. Troy, Chatham, Kent

My own name comfortably exceeds that of the gallant admiral.

(Brigadier) Dermot Hugh Blundell-Hollinshead-Blundell,
BFPO 26.

The longest multi-barrelled surname on record in England is: Major Leone Sextus Denys Oswald Fraudatifilius Tollemache-Tollemache-de-Orellana-Plantagenet-Tollemache-Tollemache (1884–1917). If you insist on non-repetitious ones, try this for size: Lady Caroline Jemima Temple-Nugent-Chandos-Brydges-Grenville (1858–1946).

Steve Arloff, Watford, Herts

If the weight of all the individuals in one species were added up, what species would come out as having the highest biomass? And would this be the most accurate way to measure a species' 'success?'

A trawl of the web suggests that nobody really knows the answer. Termites may well have three times as much biomass as humans, but as there are so many different species of termites, it doesn't help us to answer the first question. It is probable that some kind of bacterium may provide the world's greatest single-species biomass, and a good candidate would be *Prochlorococcus marinus*, the most abundant marine cyanobacterium. However, if we were to alter the question slightly and ask which animal has the greatest single-species biomass, the answer would probably be the Antarctic krill (*Euphausia superba*). Estimates of the total biomass of this crustacean range up to 1 billion tonnes, or about five times the total weight of all human beings on the planet.

Brian Bibby, London

Americans.

Lester Scott, Leicester

If you can be overwhelmed, and underwhelmed, is it possible to simply be whelmed?

Yes, if you're a mariner. At least, you could until about the sixteenth century, when it meant your ship had heeled over due to heavy seas. Overwhelmed meant capsized, turned turtle. It later acquired the more general meaning of overcome by any superior force.

The Old English verb *whelm* has become obsolete, like many other Old English (Anglo-Saxon) words that survive only in particular usages. One is *ruth*, an Old English word that was supplanted by a Norman-French word with the same meaning, pity. *Ruth* only survives in the form 'ruthless'.

Then there's hornbeam. Beam, originally *beom*, was Old English for tree (like the German *baum*), and a hornbeam was a tree whose wood was as hard as horn. Supplanted by tree, beam came to mean a tree-trunk, then a baulk of timber. Then there's slow-worm, a native British reptile that is neither slow nor a worm (it's actually a legless lizard). Slow is from an Old English word for black (found also in sloe-berry), and worm, to Angles and Saxons, meant any snake-like creature from an earthworm to a sea serpent – the slow-worm was the black serpent.

Roy Machon, Isleworth, Middx

It is possible to be leaf-whelmed, at any rate:
    Hark, hearer, hear what I do; lend a thought now,
      make believe
    We are leaf-whelmed somewhere with the hood
    Of some branchy bunchy bushybowered wood
        ('Epithalamion', Gerard Manley Hopkins)

Emily Jeremiah, London SE4

I've always wondered if, being that to be disgruntled is to be unhappy about something, can you be 'gruntled'?

Ian Noble, Loughton, Essex

Of course it is, just as it is possible to be gormful, turn up to work perfectly shevelled, perform feckfully while being ruthful to competitors, and finally drive home reckfully at the end of a hapful day to enjoy some absolutely gusting food while feeling truly gruntled and traught about it all! It's just that life, sadly, isn't often like that.

S. Nashef, Brampton, Cambs

In P. G. Wodehouse's *The Code of the Woosters*, Jeeves is unhappy because Bertie refuses to go on a round-the-world cruise. 'He spoke with a certain what-is-it in his voice, and I could see that, if not actually disgruntled, he was far from being gruntled.' Jeeves got his way in the end.

Peter Lowthian, Marlow, Bucks

Are we still evolving or is this as good as we get?

The advent of genetic engineering will allow us to fast-forward the rate of evolution and shape our progeny according to our whims. Regardless of whether this is desirable, it is uncontrollable and only a matter of time before this technology transforms humanity.

Some scientists such as Hans Moravec go even further, and suggest that a 'genetic takeover' is under way, where artificial, computerized life forms will start to evolve faster than their organic counterparts. Aided by us and unfettered by biological constraints, these programs will develop intelligence in advance of our own. Rather than being wiped out by our creations, we will be able to copy our brain patterns on to computers and transcend our bodies, 'becoming' these cybernetic super-beings.

Chris Mungall, Edinburgh

No answer is possible. Evolution is a classic example of a chaotic process – with a touch of catastrophe theory thrown in. Each micro-step is rational, but the future state is unpredictable from any knowledge we can attain of the present state.

We can, of course, speculate. We could say that man is a recent arrival on the scene, embodying exciting new developments, with lots of potential. He lacks features that species that have been around for significant evolutionary time have – for example the ability to control his population – but these deficiencies may be balanced by his ability to use intelligent behaviour to solve physiological problems in a fraction of the time biological adaptation would take.

On the other hand, the current view is that evolution proceeds in surges that follow mass extinctions caused by such events as comets hitting the earth. It is not too difficult to imagine that the next mass extinction may be due to human action and will include man. That would not actually be unprecedented. When algae discovered photosynthesis and filled the earth's atmosphere with oxygen, pre-existing anaerobic organisms, had they been articulate, must have described this as a dreadful catastrophe, and they ceased to be the dominant life forms. We, however, looking back, see the event as 'good'. There seems to be a principle at work, which we do not understand, that causes physical and biological evolution to proceed toward greater complexity and in some sense 'forward'. (St Paul had the insight that 'All things are moving toward perfection'.) I think our knowledge of the earth's history justifies optimism, whatever the future of our particular species.

(Prof.) Romaine Hervey, Wells, Somerset

If there were an ice age next week, with massive crop failures, famines and a general 'collapse of civilisation', then you can be certain that evolutionary pressures would once again come to bear. People more able to tolerate the cold (large and fat?) would be more likely to survive to breeding age; very hairy men (and women), who might be sexually unattractive now, would quickly establish a foothold in the gene pool.

David Gibson, Leeds

Why doesn't my dishwasher have a window in its door so I can see what's going on inside it like my washing machine has?

How else would you know which one you were buying?

Ian Tanner, Peterborough

You don't really want to see your crockery and metal pots on a fast spin.

Dan Usiskin, London N1

Dear questioner, for the sake of your sanity, please give serious consideration to taking up a more interesting hobby.

Linda Gresham, Birmingham

I read recently that an excessive accumulation of fat around the waist increases the risk of heart disease and that a woman's waist measurement should ideally not exceed 32 in. If I were to have the fat cells around my waist and abdomen removed, say via liposuction, would my risk of heart disease be reduced?

Overweight and obesity are associated with many health problems such as diabetes and heart disease. Waist circumference is a measure of central fat that resides under the skin, but the more important lies around the intestines and is called omental fat. The association of disease and mortality is closer with central fat (around the waist) than peripheral fat (in the arms and legs). Indeed, increased waist circumference is more important than being overweight.

The mechanisms for this association are unclear. When triglyceride, the main energy store in fat cells, is broken down, it releases fatty acids into the blood. Blood from our intestines goes via the liver before reaching the general circulation. The fatty acids from omental fat cells have the opportunity to alter our metabolism much more than those elsewhere in the body (omental fat is metabolically more active than peripheral fat.)

The removal of omental fat from rats improves their metabolism. Liposuction would remove subcutaneous fat and hopefully leave your intestines alone! Therefore, the metabolically dangerous fat would be left untouched. Furthermore, fat stores will re-accumulate unless energy intake is reduced and/or energy expenditure increased.

There are no trials of liposuction to investigate whether this would reduce the chance of heart attacks. The safer and evidence-based approach to reduce the risk of heart disease includes stopping smoking, reducing high blood pressure and treating high cholesterol and diabetes. Reducing high waist circumference probably reduces your risk of future heart disease. The way to do this is to eat less and exercise more.

Stephen Robinson, consultant physician and senior lecturer,
Unit of Metabolic Medicine, Paddington hospital, London

Why is it acceptable in modern British society to be derogatory about people with red hair?

Jealousy. Go to www.redandproud.com, click on famous redheads and find out why.

Sandy Breck-Paterson, Paussac, France

According to psychological theory, people in one group (e.g. those with brown hair) tend to talk down to people in another group (e.g. those with red hair) in order to make themselves feel better. Since more people have brown hair than red, redheads are more likely to feel the brunt of this psychological phenomenon than brown-haired folk. Incidentally, this effect is probably partly responsible for blonde jokes too, although blonde hair is also associated with youth and therefore attractiveness – which may be why blondes don't suffer as much criticism as redheads. Or it could be something to do with wee Jimmie Krankie?

Katherine Woolf, London

No, it's actually because of Chris Evans.

Antony Bellingall, Norwich

It seems as genetically unlikely that a random human being will be born beautiful as that the

same human will be born highly intelligent. Why, then, is it so much more acceptable to sneer at the attractive but idiotic (Jessica Simpson, for example) than to sneer at the intelligent but ugly (the majority of Western writers, philosophers etc.). Surely the former's gift is just as incredible?

The questioner assumes that beauty and intelligence are both wholly innate, biological traits that simply happen or don't. True, someone who is beautiful obviously got lucky in the genetics department, as opposed to someone who is average. But intelligence is much more complex than simply a case of having the right genes. It involves curiosity, lateral thinking, the ability to absorb facts, ask the right questions, reason logically, and so on.

Many of these traits can be learnt. It's possible to become intelligent even if you don't consider yourself especially brainy, but it might take a good deal of time, effort and hard thinking — and those are generally traits that are admired in society. Conversely, there's not much you can do to make yourself beautiful short of slapping on the pancake and/or plastic surgery.

There is also, of course, the question of how you define beauty. But that's for someone else to discuss.

Ed Ricketts, Bath

I resent the implication that the majority of Western philosophers are ugly.

Ross Cameron, Department of Philosophy,
University of St Andrews, Fife, Scotland

Why is life so hard?

The pithy but much quoted answer is: 'compared to what'? In truth, however, compared to any other period of human history, life has never been so easy for so many, by almost any measure one cares to apply – nutrition, healthcare, material goods, life expectancy, security, availability of travel, social mobility, access to education, entertainment, leisure time . . . the list goes on. Granted, the majority of these benefits are concentrated in the developed West. They are, nevertheless, available to many millions of people.

If you think life is hard now, you should read what it was like for the urban working classes 150 years ago.

Mike Kinley, Liverpool

The Chinese got it right all those years ago. Everything is Yin and Yang (opposites). You can't have right without left, up without down, hot without cold, good without bad, happy without sad, etc. On their own, they would be meaningless. There has to be a comparison against which to judge what we perceive.

This 'life' is the comparison with which we are able to judge our next existence (which is our real existence). In our next existence we are in a constant state of love and bliss. But if we had experienced nothing else, how would we know? What would we have, with which to compare our blissful state?

This life is that comparison: Yin and Yang. And, no, we are not here to 'learn', to enable us to go to the 'next level'. We already know the answers to every question. We are here to remember who we really are.

John Read, Birmingham

Within the framework of existential psychotherapy, experiencing life engages with the major concerns confronted in living as an aware human being. The eminent psychiatrist Irvin Yalom describes these as Death, Freedom, Isolation and Meaninglessness. Rather than a bleak template for existing, the work involved in embracing my own mortality, taking responsibility for my life, accepting that consequent isolation while constantly creating meaning out of chaos makes life hard yet also exhilarating. The experiences also quicken and deepen relating my humanity with that of others.

Jimmy McGhee, Canterbury, Kent

Because it is a beautiful diamond.

James Bradley, London SW4

HISTORICAL PEOPLE

Did Napoleon ever say 'Not tonight, Josephine'?
If not, who did?

Although it is impossible to be certain, it is highly likely that this was said at Fontainebleu on 24 October 1809. At the time, Napoleon had decided to divorce Josephine to marry the Archduchess Maria Louisa of Austria. I cannot do better than quote from R. H. Horne's *History of Napoleon* (1884, vol II): 'Napoleon had rested at Fontainebleu on his way to Paris from the campaign of Wagram. He was quickly joined by Josephine, who hastened from Saint Cloud, with her usual eagerness to welcome him. She perceived a certain restraint and embarrassment in his manner towards her, and found the doors of communication between their apartments entirely closed; these were the first intimations she received of the approach of an event which had long haunted her imagination.'

D. Wardley, Halesowen, West Mids

What was the last recorded instance of a duel being fought with seconds, at ten paces and using pistols?

My ancestor, Captain George Cadogan, avoided the police to fight a duel with pistols and seconds on Wimbledon Common on 30 May 1809. His opponent, Lord Paget, had seduced George's sister Charlotte, who was married to the Duke of Wellington's brother. The duel was fought at twelve paces, not ten, and they both missed (in Lord Paget's case this was deliberate).

David Colombi, Angmering, West Sussex

The Duke of Wellington fought a duel with pistols, and seconds, on 21 March 1829. His opponent was Lord Winchilsea, who had cast a public slur on Wellington's political honour. They met at Battersea Fields. The seconds were Sir Henry Hardinge and Lord Falmouth respectively. The duel was fought at twelve paces, and as the command 'Fire' was given, Wellington noticed that Winchilsea kept his arm close to his side. The Duke fired wide, accordingly, and Winchilsea fired in the air. A brief letter of apology was presented by Hardinge, and the matter was deemed concluded. (Source: *Wellington – Pillar Of State*, Elizabeth Longford, 1972.)

Carol Ball, Aylesford, Kent

On 19 October 1852, in a duel with seconds, Emanuel Barthelemy shot and killed Frederic Cournet on Priests Hill, Egham, Surrey. The full ceremony was observed, with the combatants standing back-to-back and walking twenty paces before turning and firing.

Duncan Mirylees, Guildford

In December 1971 a duel was fought between a Uruguayan field marshal and a general, after the former had dubbed his colleague 'a socialist'. The protagonists met at dawn in a Montevideo public park and, from twenty-five paces, fired thirty-eight rounds at each other. Neither was hurt. According to the field marshal's second, the men did not put on their glasses before commencing the back-to-back walk. (Source: *The Book Of Heroic Failures*, Stephen Pile, 1979.)

Dominic Gould, Hull

Is it true that Dick Turpin was buried standing upright? If so, why?

This false story probably comes from the fact that Turpin was buried in a very deep grave, in the churchyard of St George's parish in York. Turpin was a popular villain and, according to Benson's *Remarkable Trials And Notorious Characters* (*c.* 1842), 'the people who acted as mourners took such measures as they thought would secure the body.'

The body was illegally exhumed the next morning and eventually found in a surgeon's garden. Turpin was reburied in the same grave.

Mike Meakin, London SW19

He had a dyslexic gravedigger who thought his name was Dick Turnip.

Terry Mahoney, Buntingford, Herts

I have heard that Siegfried Sassoon and Robert Graves fell out because of their First-World-War experiences. Is this true?

The friendship between Graves and Sassoon did not break down because of their war experiences. The relevant occasion was the publication in 1929 of *Goodbye To All That*. In the original text Graves had included, in breach of copyright, a hitherto unpublished poem that Sassoon had sent him privately years earlier, and which he did not want printed. Graves had also made certain references to Sassoon's mother that were thought unacceptable.

These passages were deleted at the printers, but not before some copies of the book in its original form, numbering perhaps a hundred or so, had got through. The bulk of the edition contains two or three cancelled pages filled with printed asterisks in lieu of text.

(Dr) T. Kramer, London

Dr Kramer tells only part of the story. Sassoon and Graves frequently fell out with one another. In 1917 Sassoon, a serving officer, made a public anti-war statement, hoping to be court-martialled. To protect Sassoon Graves testified to Sassoon's insanity. Sassoon was found not responsible for his action and sent for treatment to Craiglockhart hospital, Edinburgh, but came to resent Graves' role. Their row went on for ten years, culminating in the publication of Graves' *Goodbye To All That*. Sassoon was unhappy about how he and his anti-war statement were depicted and forbade Graves from using his copyright material. In his war memoirs, published soon after Graves's, Sassoon called Graves 'a fad-ridden crank'.

Peter Brooke, Aberdeen

Why was James VI of Scotland (I of England) dubbed 'the wisest fool in Christendom' by Henri IV of France?

The observation was first published in England by Sir Anthony Weldon in his *The Court And Character Of King James*, in 1650 (during the interregnum when such sentiments passed the censor). Weldon hated James, who expelled him from court in 1625. He wrote: 'He was very crafty and cunning in petty things . . . inasmuch as a very wise man was wont to say, he believed him the very wisest fool in Christendom.'

It is uncertain whether this 'very wise man' was the Duc de Sully, Henri IV's finance minister, and close friend and battle companion, or the King of France himself. The original appraisal is most likely to date from 1603, when Henri sent Sully as ambassador to England on James's accession. Sully would then have reported his impressions of the new king, resulting in an exchange such as: 'Sire, the King of England is a fool.' 'In that case, Sully, he is the wisest fool in Christendom.' In any case, it cannot be any later than 1610, when Henri IV was assassinated, and I imagine that Henri was too busy from 1589 to 1598 fighting the Catholic League for his right to the throne to consider James.

The oxymoronic jibe suggests that though James was extremely learned, and a published author, in the practice of rulership he could be extremely foolish. But perhaps this foolishness was a mask. Weldon wrote that James's private motto was 'Qui nescit dissimulare, nescit regnare' (He who does not know how to dissimulate does not know how to reign). Perhaps James, like Hamlet, was merely putting on an antic disposition – playing the fool for his own purposes.

Miranda Kaufman, London NW2

King James's famous conclusion to his polemic against tobacco smoking shows some degree of wisdom: 'A custom loathsome to the eye, hateful to the nose, harmful to the brain, dangerous to the lungs, and in the black stinking fume thereof nearest resembles the horrible Stygian gloom of the Pit that is bottomless.'

Gerald McAreavey, Culcheth, Cheshire

James VI was no fool. He or his courtiers brought golf to England.

Mike Chambers, Peterborough

If Guy Fawkes had lit the gunpowder, would it really have killed King James I and his parliament, or just given them a bit of a fright?

The short answer is that the king and those with him would probably have been killed. Although superseded by more powerful explosives, black gunpowder was, by the time of the plot, sufficiently evolved to be a very dangerous commodity indeed. Ignited en masse, in a cellar, it would lack the shattering effect of modern high explosives but it would certainly have caused extensive demolition, probably accompanied by fire. Black gunpowder is still a very popular explosive in quarries in various parts of the world.

(Dr) M. Rasburn, near Whittington, Chesterfield, Derbys

Why are pirates invariably depicted with eye-patches and wooden legs? Was there a higher incidence of industrial injury in their line of work, or were they just clumsy?

There was a high rate of such industrial injuries in all sea-faring between the middle of the seventeenth century and the end of the Napoleonic wars (the period featured in Hollywood swashbucklers). It could hardly have been otherwise.

The most common form of sea engagement during that period seems to have been the medium or close-range firing of cannon broadside on, at or between vessels. On to and into those ships came smashing cannonballs, which, when they did not decapitate or otherwise kill outright, lopped off limbs, or at least smashed them so destructively that the only chance for survival was prompt amputation. Cannonades brought down heavy timber on and through decks – more crushing injuries, more amputations – and turned the wood of a ship into cutting projectiles.

If muskets were used at closer range, a heavy musket-ball was at least as likely to smash a limb (needing amputation) as to pierce it. And in hand-to-hand combat to secure a ship, the cutlass was common, because as a slashing weapon it could be used with the minimum of footwork, in tight conditions. The result: more severing injuries, and also vertical cuts to the forehead and down through the eye-area.

Although soldiers during the same era faced similar dangers, the concentration of fire on the relatively small, man-filled target of a ship must have meant sailors/pirates had a very high chance of mutilation, and an even bigger one of death. And at sea, it isn't easy to run away.

Ann MacDonald, London

The main cause, surely, was the type of artillery in use. Eighteenth-century cannons were loaded with coarse black gunpowder, and fired by putting some of the powder in a hole at the back of the gun and lighting it with a slow match. Although most of the powder would blast forward, an appreciable proportion would vent out through the touch-hole. Anyone firing a cannon was therefore very likely to get a blast of burning powder in the face, with a grave risk of eye injury.

A smooth-bored gun, firing a roughly rounded shot with poor quality powder from a moving ship would only have an accurate range of a few yards. It was probably customary to fire a broadside practically at the point of contact. At that range a cannonball fired into the side of a wooden ship would scatter large jagged splinters of wood about the deck. Anyone receiving a wound in the body would probably die of gangrene within a few days. Gangrene could be prevented in a limb injury, however, by rapid removal of the limb (first partially anaesthetising the patient with rum or laudanum – a solution of opium and rum), tying up the cut arteries and cauterising the stump in hot tar. Anyone who survived the immediate traumatic effect of this treatment would probably escape gangrenous infection, but would have to make use of a prosthetic device such as a hook or wooden leg.

Martin Guha, London SE3

Once you've got a shiny new hook for a hand, you'll discover why an eye-patch is needed when you attempt to rub your eye.

Bridget Savage, Bexley, Kent

At what event did Queen Victoria say: 'We are not amused?'

A royal pooch that had not been properly palace trained made a puddle on the carpet. This brought an indulgent smile to the lips of a number of people present until Her Majesty uttered these words, whereupon all faces promptly became straight. The Queen's remark, rather than the puddle, illustrates what is meant by 'the royal we'.

Michael J. Smith, Norfolk

According to *Brewer's Dictionary of Phrase & Fable*, this was a reproof attributed to Queen Victoria when a groom-in-waiting, Alexander Graham Yorke, allegedly imitated her. However, there appears to be no evidence that she ever used the expression.

Susan Curtis, Manchester

Lions have been used in British heraldry since the 1100s. Who in Britain at that time would have seen a lion and how?

Don't underestimate how much people travelled – 1100 is as yesterday in human terms. People have always traded and communicated. The Romans were here for centuries and must have been well aware of what lions were like, since they threw them to the gladiators.

Vivienne Cox, London

Lions still lived in North Africa, the Near East and Southern Europe until the late nineteenth century. They were well known to the Romans. They get Bible references – Daniel in the lion's den, for example. So while I doubt that many peasants would have seen a lion, they would probably have been aware of them, and capable of recognising even a Norman depiction of one.

Richard Miller, Addlestone, Surrey

Harry Houdini, the escapologist, wrote down the secrets of his escapes and had the letters sealed in a bank vault, not to be opened until twenty-five years after his death. Have they now been opened?

Like the story that Houdini drowned during a failed escape from his notorious Chinese Water Torture Cell, this delicious rumour is untrue. Houdini was never coy about his methods: he was an obsessive note-keeper and his writings on escapology were frequently published during his lifetime. As a magician myself, I would be made to eat worms by my colleagues if I were to give details here, but for anyone genuinely interested, *The Secrets Of Houdini* by J. C. Cannell (first published in 1931, just five years after Houdini's death, and reissued in 1973 by Dover Publications) gives a comprehensive account. However, I warn readers that this is a dreary technical book. The real secret of Houdini's success was his mastery of showmanship, and a clever manipulation of the press for maximum publicity.

Tom Cutler, Hove, East Sussex

Edward the Confessor ruled England from 1041 to 1066, and there had been two previous kings of the English with the same name, yet it is the fourth

ruler of England named Edward, (reigned 1272–1307) who is counted as Edward I. Why?

In the Middle Ages, the numbering of kings was not well established, and distinguishing one from another was a matter of convenience rather than logic. At first, when King Edward (1272–1307) needed to be distinguished from other King Edwards, he was referred to as King Edward son of King Henry, and his son was similarly called Edward son of King Edward. When the latter's son succeeded, to avoid reciting a long pedigree, he was described as King Edward the third after the conquest of England (*a conquestu Angliae*), and henceforth this system was applied to his father and grandfather as well. Thus the present numbering arises out of having three Edwards in turn following two centuries of an Edward-free throne.

M. G. Snape, Durham

What's so terrible about snake-oil salesmen? Why have they become a byword for untrustworthy conmen?

Snake meat contains almost no fat, so snake oil does not exist. A snake-oil salesman is therefore a synonym for a con artist.

David Gibson, Leeds

One would think that snake meat contains little fat, snakes being cold-blooded, but Slavomir Rawicz describes in *The Long Walk* crossing the Gobi desert and surviving on snakes: 'The clear fat which oozed out over the heat of the fire we used as a balm for our lips, our sore eyes and our feet, and the soothing effect lasted for hours.'

Jeremy Light, Mens, France

David Gibson is logical – but wrong. The oil in question is oil in which a snake has been marinading. It is (alleged) to be efficacious for almost all ills, whether taken internally or applied externally. Such salesmen are to be seen in Japan, at the monthly flea markets in Toji temple, Kyoto, for example. The snake is a *mamushi* – a kind of viper, and poisonous – also to be seen, dried, in the windows of old-fashioned shops selling traditional medicine. I have often seen these salesmen surrounded by eager crowds, with handfuls of cash, ready to buy: there's one born every minute!

Richard Lock, Quebec, Canada

What is the point of string vests? Who invented them? Are they fashionable?

In the war museum at Arromanches in Normandy, there is a string vest that, I think, is fifteen metres long. This was issued to RAF pilots in the Second World War to be worn under their tunics. The purpose, we are told, was that in the unlikely event of finding themselves stranded in the top of a tree after being shot down, they could let it out and use it to climb down.

This raises the questions: did you undress at the top of the tree? What happened if you were a few metres short? Did anyone ever use his string vest?

K. Roberts, Durham

During the Second World War, I served with the 52nd 'Mountain' Division Scotland. Among the special clothing issued to me was a string vest. Wearing this helped to keep the body warm in winter (through the thermal effect of many small areas of trapped air), and cool in summer. I imagine the vest was probably invented by a Norwegian. For fifty-three years since the war, I have always worn 100 per cent cotton string vests manufactured by a firm called Brynje of Larvik, Norway.

Name withheld

Albert Einstein received a Nobel prize for his 1905 explanation of the photoelectric effect but no such recognition for his work on special and general relativity, the theories on which his fame is based. Why not?

Einstein was nominated for the Nobel prize in physics every year from 1910 to 1922 except for 1911 and 1915. In most cases he was nominated for his work on both special and general relativity. Historians of science have given two reasons why Einstein never received the prize for special and general relativity. First these theories were so revolutionary that the scientists on the awarding committee simply didn't understand them well enough at the time to pass judgment and were concerned that not all his predictions had been experimentally verified. Second it is said that certain anti-Semitic members of the Swedish Academy of Sciences awarding committee were influenced by the lobbying of the German physicist Philipp Lenard, later to become a Nazi, who claimed that relativity was a counterintuitive, non-Aryan and Jewish theory.

However, the spectacular confirmation of Einstein's general theory in 1919, when light from distant stars was shown to be deflected by the gravitational influence of the sun, made him the first scientific superstar and the Swedish Academy could no longer ignore him. His 1922 Nobel Prize citation read: 'For his services to theoretical physics and especially for his discovery of the law of the photoelectric effect.' The letter to Einstein from the secretary of the Academy added: 'but without taking into account the value which will be accorded your relativity and gravitation theories after these are confirmed in the future'. Einstein was awarded the prize for his quantum theory explanation of the photoelectric effect, published in 1905. The irony is that this phenomenon was discovered by Lenard for which he was awarded the 1905 Nobel physics prize. Lenard's virulent anti-Semitism prevented him from ever accepting Einstein's quantum explanation for the effect.

Reg Dennick, Nottingham

When, and why, did men first start shaving? At face value, it seems ludicrous to scrape hair off the body every day.

Alexander the Great is responsible. The rationale behind its introduction was that an enemy soldier could gain an advantage by seizing his opponent by the beard. I don't know if there are any records of soldiers being killed in this way in classical times. Mary Renault, in her book *The Nature Of Alexander*, suggests that his real motive was to preserve his own androgynous appearance; the practice then spread to his men.

Alan Dimes, London SW10

They started long before Alexander the Great. He lived in the fourth century BC, but sculptures from the ancient civilisations of Mesopotamia, the Nile and the Indus show

that members of the Sumerian, Egyptian and Indian rul-
ing classes were clean-shaven 2,000–3,000 years earlier.

Nicolas Walter, London N1

**What is the origin of the rather idiosyncratic
names of some types of biscuits, such as garibaldi?**

Garibaldi biscuits were invented by Huntley & Palmer in
1864 and put on the market in that year when Giuseppe
Garibaldi visited this country. He received an ecstatic welcome, as is described in chapter 21 of my book, *The Lion
Of Caprera*, and the whole country, apart from Queen
Victoria and Karl Marx, rose to greet him. Incidentally,
while I was correcting the proofs of my book in the sun
outside a hotel in Spain a teacher from an American
school asked me what I was doing. I told her I had just
written a new biography of Garibaldi. There was a silence
until she said brightly, 'Oh yes, the biscuit manufacturer'.

John Parris, Abingdon, Oxon

**Is there any truth in the story that a British officer
in the First World War would not allow his troops
to wear helmets because he thought they were
'sissy'?**

In *The First Day On The Somme*, Martin Middlebrook writes that the steel helmet was first issued in the spring of 1916. It apparently reduced head wounds by 75 per cent, but 'one divisional commander, who also forbade the issue of rum, refused at first to permit the use of steel helmets. He considered that it would encourage the men to go soft.' Such was the calibre of leadership that left nearly 20,000 British men dead on the first day of that battle.

Paul Flint, Madrid, Spain

Why was Lee Harvey Oswald, the alleged assassin of President Kennedy in 1963, allowed to visit the Soviet Union at height of the cold war, marry a Russian national and return, at a time when those attempting to flee from East Germany were shot?

A good question, and one that has puzzled agents of Cuban security ever since the assassination of Kennedy. Recently declassified material in Cuba shows that shortly before the assassination, a person calling himself Lee Harvey Oswald had appeared at the Cuban embassy in Mexico City and had tried to get a visa to visit Havana. The event was recorded in the embassy log because the person had apparently caused a scene when he was told he would have to wait thirty days for authorization, insisting that he was the head of the New Orleans Free Cuba

Committee and had important information to give to Fidel Castro.

Enquiries into the New Orleans Free Cuba Committee by Cuban agents revealed that this was a bogus outfit with no connections to the real Cuba friendship movement in the US at the time. All this led Cuban security to believe that had the person calling himself Lee Harvey Oswald been successful in visiting Havana, a case could have been made to link Cuba to the crime and therefore provide a pretext to invade the island. Readers interested in learning more about this should read Claudia Furiati's *ZR Rifle: The Plot To Kill Kennedy And Castro* (Ocean Press).

(Dr) Stephen Wilkinson, London N1

The answer is provided by Allen Dulles, who was head of the CIA until J. F. K. sacked him over the Bay of Pigs debacle. In his book *The Craft Of Intelligence*, published by Harper & Row in 1963, some months before Oswald came to prominence as Kennedy's alleged assassin, Dulles devotes part of chapter nine to 'phoney defectors':

The phoney 'defector', when interviewed by persons in the country to which he has 'defected', may pick up and be able to send back a certain amount of information, especially concerning what is known or not known about his own country. A further and final step in such phoney defections is that the defector may eventually 'redefect'. One day he will announce that he is disillusioned . . . he repents of his sins and wants to go home even if he is to be punished for his original defection. This provides some propaganda repercussion, is embarrassing to the country of haven, and is a convenient way for the defector, who was really an agent, to return home and report on the information he has been assembling.

No, I don't think Oswald shot Kennedy, but he moved in circles where he could all too easily have been fitted up for the role.

B. J. Burden, Bocking, Essex

The most plausible explanation yet, backed by compelling evidence from several sources, was that Oswald was used by US naval intelligence (he was a specialist US Marine Corps air traffic radar operator stationed at a base in Japan from which U2 spy planes took off and landed) in a fake defector programme they were running against the Soviet Union.

The idea was to see if fake defectors could be infiltrated into the Soviet intelligence set-up as double agents. At the time of Oswald's 'defection', such programmes were being run separately by all three major US armed services without knowledge of each other's activities. Most of these attempts proved futile as the Soviet intelligence and security apparatus proved more adept at spotting the fakes than the US intelligence apparatus was at creating them.

The most plausible explanation as to why Oswald married a Russian girl called Marina was that the 'accidental' way they met at a dance in Minsk in 1961 was not accidental at all: Marina was told to befriend and marry Oswald by the KGB. She would then live with him and report back to the KGB on everything Oswald said or did while he remained in the Soviet Union. This appears to have been standard KGB policy with all defectors who they felt might be of dubious origin.

As a straightforward low-grade informer and not a trained KGB agent, she would have been of no interest to the CIA or FBI when she and Oswald were granted entry visas to the US (in suspiciously trouble-free, record time) after Oswald's bluff had been called by the KGB.

All of this and more besides can be found in the thoroughly researched, soundly argued and pretty near definitive book *The Kennedy Conspiracy* by Anthony Summers.

Howard Avis, Rugby, Warks

Who was the last person to be beheaded in this country? Was an official decision made to stop the practice?

Simon, Lord Lovat, was the last person beheaded in England, on 9 April 1747. Beheading is said to have been introduced into England by William the Conqueror in the eleventh century, and the punishment was usually reserved for offenders of high rank. The fourth Earl Ferrers was hanged after a petition (1760) to be beheaded was refused.

In 1814 the King of England was empowered by royal warrant to substitute hanging as the ordinary method of executing criminals. Yet beheading remained part of the common law method of dealing with treason as late as 1820: traitors had their heads cut off by a masked man after they were hanged.

Tony Martin, London SE15

Who first described aristocratic blood as 'blue', and why?

The Arab Moors subjugated Spain in the early part of the eighth century. The indigenous Spaniards possessed relatively pale complexions, and intermarriages between the Moors and Spaniards resulted in a gradual darkening of the 'typical' Iberian skin. The Spanish aristocracy, doing their best to avoid the Moors, removed themselves to northern enclaves such as Aragon and Castille. It is thought they went as far as shunning the sun in order to

heighten their chromodermal uniqueness. So the aristo-
crats developed very white skin, through which veins
were clearly visible. Dark red venous blood appears blue
through skin, therefore, these well-bred Spaniards were
handed the moniker of Blue Bloods (*de Sangre Azul*).

Mike Fisher, Tadworth, Surrey

**During Captain Bligh's 4,000-mile voyage with
nineteen people crowded into an open launch,
it rained almost non-stop. To avoid hypothermia,
he had everyone soak his or her clothing in the
seawater, wring it out and put it on. For the rest
of his life he maintained that this strategy saved
their lives. What, if anything, was happening to
protect them?**

In 1951 I took part in the trials in the Johor Strait of the
tented, automatically inflated life-rafts developed by the
Royal Navy. Over most of the world's seas, cold is the
most urgent threat to castaways' survival but in the tropics
(where virtually all long voyages took place) the problem
is loss of body water. This is greatly increased by sweating. We found that instructing the volunteers in the rafts
to keep their clothes continuously wet with sea water during the daytime, together with the other aspects of the
raft drill, was totally effective in countering sweating: that

is, it reduced loss of water from the body by evaporation to exactly the level seen in the same subjects in an ideal environment in the laboratory.

As compared with the worst case – survivors in an open craft exposed to the tropical sun and with no fresh water – expected survival time would be increased from two to three days to two to three weeks. Some rain is usually available in the tropics but unless there are effective means of collecting it (such as the life-raft provides), for really long voyages it is likely to sustain only a small number of survivors.

Romaine Hervey, Wells, Avon

The 1989 book *The Hangman's Tale: Memoirs Of A Public Executioner* refers to the hanging of twenty-two American servicemen during the war, at Shepton Mallet in Somerset. How common were such wartime executions? For what crimes had the men been sentenced? How many of them were black?

The Shepton Mallet hangings were one of many stories about American GIs in Britain. Another was that hospitals in the Bristol area were packed with 'brown babies' – the offspring of white British women and black GIs.

Wartime censorship helped to create rumours by

default but in this instance the Visiting Forces Act of 1942 was a cause of speculation because it gave the American military authorities exclusive criminal jurisdiction over their armed forces in Britain. Moreover, the American military code specified that rape carried a sentence of death or imprisonment for life, when it was not a capital offence in Britain. This became an issue both inside and outside parliament in 1944 when there was a feeling that black GIs were being treated by the American authorities more harshly than their white colleagues.

Statistics about sentences were notoriously difficult to obtain but some were produced by US Judge Advocate General Edwin McNeil in June 1944. By that date in the European Theatre of Operations eight white and ten black Americans had been convicted of rape. Of these, one black serviceman had been executed (though he had also committed a murder) and five were sentenced to life imprisonment. No whites had been executed for rape, though two had been given life sentences. In addition, four white and ten black servicemen were found guilty of murder. Of these, two white men were executed and one given life, whereas five black men were executed and three given life. In addition, both black and white GIs lost their lives in incidents of inter-racial violence in Britain.

Graham A. Smith, (author of When Jim Crow Met John Bull – Black American Soldiers In World War II Britain)*, Wolverhampton*

I once read that the Americans had intercepted several radio transmissions made by dying Russian cosmonauts before Yuri Gagarin's successful spaceflight. Any confirmation?

Copies of *The Guinness Book Of Records* printed in the early sixties contained a list of 'Soviet space fatalities' from *c.* 1957 to 1960. On various dates, named cosmonauts were alleged to have asphyxiated, gone mad in orbit, burned up on re-entry, survived but been consigned to mental institutions, etc.

I have never seen mention of this list or these 'facts' anywhere else. Glasnost within the Soviet space programme and eager digging by Western journalists should have revealed a pattern of disaster by now if any existed. I assume the editors of the *Book Of Records* were fed a straight piece of anti-Soviet propaganda and fell for it.

J. T. Brooks, Rogerstone, Gwent

Who exactly were Tom, Dick and Harry?

They were all members of the Dunsden family from Fulbrook in Oxfordshire, a village close to Burford of Levellers fame. The nearby village of Icomb was an island of Worcestershire surrounded by the county of Gloucestershire, of which it has been part since 1844. Its status meant that it was a popular area for various rogues to operate from across the county boundary into Gloucestershire and Oxfordshire. Tom, Dick and Harry's most famous exploit was a raid on the Gloucester mail. Tom and Harry were subsequently arrested and hanged in Gloucester in 1785. Their bodies were taken to, and shown from, the Gibbet Oak near to Fulbrook. Dick was never captured.

John Wilson, Oxford

The famous American film producer, Sam Goldwyn, was once told that an actress contracted to his studio had had a baby. Goldwyn asked what she had called the child. John, he was told. Goldwyn's reported response was: 'What kind of name is John? Why, every Tom, Dick and Harry's called John.'

Rhys Williams, Cwmann, Lampeter

Tom was 'strong as a bear and two yards long'. Dick was 'big as a barrel and three feet thick'. Harry was 'six feet tall and sweet as a cherry'. All were lovers of Polly Garter, although the one she 'loved best was little Willy Wee and he's six feet deep'. (See *Under Milk Wood*, Dylan Thomas.)

George Kitchin, Tirril, Penrith

John Wilson's story of the Oxfordshire rogues is incorrect. Shakespeare in *Henry IV* (1597) has 'Tom, Dick and

Francis' in this sense, and we all know who Old Harry was. *The Oxford Dictionary of Idioms* also has 'Farewell, Tom, Dick and Harry. Farewell, Moll, Nell and Sue.' The surname version is 'Brown, Jones and Robinson' (*Brewer's Dictionary of Phrase & Fable*).

Brian Robinson, Hutton, Essex

The station car park at Auffay, Normandy, is named Place Michel Hollard, with the explanation that Hollard was 'l'homme qui sauva Londres en 1943'. Who was he, and how did he save London?

Michel Hollard was a French engineer who, when the Germans occupied France in 1940, escaped to Switzerland. He made contact with the British embassy there and began working for British intelligence, running a network of agents called AGIR who crossed the border to carry out espionage missions in occupied France.

In 1943, after hearing about a new factory in Normandy, Hollard and his team discovered dozens of sites across the north of France, all with concrete runways aligned towards London. Eventually, Hollard uncovered the purpose of these sites – the V1 'flying bomb'. Hollard and his agents infiltrated the plants and stole blueprints to send back to England. He is commemorated at Auffay, because it was there at the railway station that Hollard, disguised as a railway worker, examined one of the bombs and made detailed descriptions of it. He also found out where one of the V1 designers was staying and had the RAF bomb the place, killing the scientist.

Using AGIR's vital information, the Allies were able to destroy many of the V1 launch sites and factories. Although the 'Doodlebugs' caused much death and destruction in London in the later years of the war, the damage would have been far greater if not for the heroic work of Hollard and his network.

Hollard continued his espionage work until he was betrayed and arrested by the Gestapo in 1944. He was tortured but refused to talk and eventually escaped when the ship he was being held in was bombed and sank. At the end of the war he was decorated by both France and Britain and quietly returned to his profession as an engineer. He died in 1993, aged ninety-five. His story is told in George Martelli's book, *The Man Who Saved London*.

Duncan Harris, Chesterfield, Derbys

Who was the last Western head of state to fight in battle?

The last British monarch to lead troops into battle was George II at the Battle of Dettingen in 1743 during the War of the Austrian Succession. On mainland Europe,

Napoleon III commanded at the Battle of Sedan in 1870, and there is a sad vignette of him in Zola's *Le Débacle*, trying to expose himself to fire so that he might be shot and not survive his defeat. The latest clear example seems to be General Pilsudski, President of Poland 1918–22, who commanded troops during the Russo-Polish war of 1920. In other cases the head of state is usually too remote from the actual conflict to qualify reasonably.

The last European ruler to die in battle seems to have been Charles XII of Sweden in 1718, although one might include F. Solano Lopez, the megalomaniac dictator of Paraguay, in 1870.

Simon Corcoran, Portsmouth

Did they ever 'shoot the messenger'? If so, how bad was the news?

The trouble is that the messenger is often implicated in the message. In the Bible (Samuel 1), an unnamed messenger brings to David news of the death in battle of his arch rival King Saul, even handing David the crown and clearly convinced that his news was good. On being interrogated, however, he admits to having killed Saul himself, albeit at the mortally wounded monarch's request. Horrified that the man had 'lifted his hand to destroy the Lord's anointed', David has the hapless messenger killed on

the spot. Even messengers have to learn discretion.
Michael J. Smith, Swaffham, Norfolk

Baha'u'llah, the founder of the Baha'i Faith, was exiled from Persia for upsetting the Muslim clergy. He was eventually imprisoned in Akka, in Palestine, by the Sultan of Turkey. From there he wrote to the Shah of Persia, 'We hope, however, that His Majesty the Shah will himself examine these matters.' The messenger, a seventeen-year-old youth, was brutally tortured to death at the instigation of the same Muslim cleric in July 1869.
(Mrs) A. Bainbridge, Flinders Island, Tasmania

Well, they crucified Christ and they shot Gandhi and Martin Luther King. How bad was the message? 'Love, equality and justice' . . . how bad can it get?
John Young, Abu Dhabi, U. A. E.

Why is St George the patron saint of England? And why is he the patron saint of Catalonia?

In his *Oxford Dictionary Of Saints*, David Hugh Farmer explains that St George was adopted as patron saint in the Middle Ages by England and Catalonia, as well as by Venice, Genoa and Portugal, because he was the personification of the ideals of Christian chivalry.

St George had been known in England since the seventh-eighth centuries but his cult gained new impetus in England during the Crusades. A vision of George and Demetrius at the siege of Antioch preceded the defeat of the Saracens and the fall of the town on the first crusade. Richard I placed himself and his army under George's protection, and St George was subsequently regarded as the special patron of soldiers. Edward III founded the Order of the Garter under St George's patronage in 1348. In 1415 – after the battle of Agincourt, when Henry V invoked George as England's patron – St George's feast was raised in rank to one of the principal feasts of the year.

St George remained popular in the post-medieval period, but as there is considerable doubt about the historical veracity of his legend, his cult was reduced to a local one in the reform of the Roman calendar in 1969.

Katherine Lewis, York

By the time George took over from Edward the Confessor as patron of England – at the founding of the Order of the Garter – he had already been guarding Doncaster for over 400 years. In the east he was generally held to protect the armies of Byzantium, and is claimed as national saint by both Georgia and Ethiopia. In Germany he is one of the 'Fourteen Saints' who are considered particularly receptive to prayers for help – and in this century was to become the favourite national image of Nazi propaganda.

George's attraction was originally as a martyr in the persecution of AD 303. Tradition elaborated his death into a highly imaginative and varied list of tortures, offering church artists a complete iconographic programme, as at St Neots in Cornwall. At the time of the crusades he also begins to be shown as a mounted dragon-slayer – a depiction probably borrowed from late Egyptian carvings of the god Horus.

Tom Hennell, Withington, Manchester

I was net-surfing and found a reference to the explorer Mungo Park, who was apparently killed either by Africans who thought his party were Muslim raiders, or eaten by zombies. Is there any truth in this, or is it tosh?

Mungo Park (1771–1806) became a doctor after undertaking medical studies at Edinburgh University. Park (presumed to have been named after St Mungo, patron saint of Glasgow), made two journeys to the interior of Africa to trace the course of the Niger River. His first journey into the Gambia started in May 1795 (see Mungo Park's *Life and Travels*, Hodder & Stoughton, *c.* 1919).

His second journey started in May 1805, with a party of forty Europeans, including thirty-five privates of the

Royal Africa Corps. During this second journey, Park and the five surviving Europeans in his party, left in a schooner to sail down the Niger from Sansanding in present-day Mali. The party was attacked by an army of the King of Haussa some thousand miles downstream from Sansanding. Park and the other Europeans are reported to have jumped into the river to escape the attack and were presumed drowned.

It is possible that the party was mistaken for Moorish raiders, whom he encountered during the first journey.

Gordon Lamond, Dalgety Bay, Fife

It is tosh. *The Life and Travels of Mungo Park*, published in the late 1860s, describes Park's death in 1805 as follows:

There is before Boussa a rock extending across the river, with only one opening in it, in the form of a door, for the water to pass through. The king's men took posses-sion of the top of this rock, until Park came up to it and attempted to pass. The natives attacked him and his friends with lances, pikes, arrows, and other missiles. Park defended himself vigorously for a long time but at last, after throwing everything in the canoe overboard, being overpow-ered by numbers, and seeing no chance of getting the canoe past, he took hold of one of the white men, and jumped into the river. Martyn did the same and the whole were drowned in their attempt to escape by swimming.

A much more mundane end than the zombie theory, brought about by the king's irritation at not having received presents from Park.

R. Creedon, Orpington, Kent

Who exactly was St Vitus and was he any good at dancing?

Vitus (the son of a pagan Sicilian senator) was converted by, and later martyred with, his nurse and her husband (Vitus's tutor). He became the patron saint of nervous disorders for casting an evil spirit out of the son of the Emperor Diocletian. In seventeenth-century Germany it was reputed that dancing in front of a statue of Vitus on his feast day (15 June) would guarantee good health for the following year. Such dancing to excess is said to have been confused with Sydenham's chorea – thus its popular name of St Vitus' dance.

Gordon A. Campbell, Dundee

The book *The People's War*, by Angus Calder, states that during the Second World War 'a schoolmaster

was jailed for advancing "defeatist" theories to his pupils'. Does anybody have any more information?

In 1940 my father was teaching in the evacuation branch of a preparatory school. In a religious knowledge lesson he said that even Hitler was as valuable in the eyes of God as anyone else. I don't know which parent shopped him, but he had a very unpleasant visit from Special Branch.

John Batts, Banbury, Oxon

In a recent book review in the *Guardian* a woman was said to have been prosecuted in 1944 under the Witchcraft Act of 1735. What did the act say, and is it still on the books?

The 1735 act repealed various earlier acts, which had set out penalties for the practice of witchcraft, and replaced them with a penalty for those who claimed to practise witchcraft and work magic, with a maximum of a year's imprisonment. The 1944 case was brought against Helen Duncan, a spiritualist, and it was the outrage generated by her subsequent conviction and imprisonment that led to the passing of the Fraudulent Mediums Act, fifty years ago this month. This not only repealed the Witchcraft Act, but recognized genuine mediumship by requiring that prosecutions could only be made against those practising mediumship 'with intent to deceive'.

One result of the repeal of the Witchcraft Act was that witches, who had been practising their religion in secret, were able to come out into the open.

Philip Heselton, Hull, East Yorks

I have heard that at the time of Suez, an RAF Canberra pilot in Cyprus, about to take off, pulled the undercarriage toggle in protest at the bombing of Port Said and the aircraft became a write-off. Is this a myth? If not, what happened to him?

The story is not a myth. The pilot had apparently requested his squadron commander not to send him on the bombing mission, since he had serious doubts about the morality of bombing targets where civilians might be killed due to what he considered a misconceived policy by Sir Anthony Eden – a judgment that has now gained considerable support. However, his squadron commander apparently insisted the pilot fulfil his role during the engagement. While lining up for take-off, the pilot retracted the undercarriage, disabling the aircraft. The pilot was subsequently court-martialled and, I believe, given eighteen months' detention, followed by dishon ourable discharge from the service. I do not believe the aircraft was damaged beyond repair, although during the Suez crisis two other Canberra bombers were lost.

Dilwyn Hardwidge (former Canberra navigator),
Cleethorpes, Lincs

Three years before this, I was standing beside a Canberra in Tripoli with the upper half of my body inside the hatch, talking to the pilot, when the same thing happened, though by accident, because his glove had caught in the undercarriage locking mechanism. I escaped being crushed by inches and emerged with only a sore head from being thumped by the hatch door as the whole thing came down. I was later assured that my suffering would not be in vain because the aircraft's controls would be modified in such a way as to make raising the under-carriage while on the ground impossible: promises, promises!

John Walsh, Swindon

I witnessed the incident at Nicosia airport. I was a corporal (instruments), serving on the pilot's City of Lincoln, 61 Squadron; the commanding officer was Squadron Leader Rooke. I don't remember the name of the pilot, but I think he was married to a member of the Guinness family. The aircraft was not a write-off; we were told to stand back while the aircraft was supported on jacks and the armourers removed the bombs. In January 1957 the aircraft, being flown by Rooke, crashed in Basingbourne (Herts) and he was killed.

Alan Wilson, Crossgates, Leeds

Many of us in the RAF at the time had similar misgivings about the operation – but the pilot's action was entirely wrong. His aircraft was carrying a full bombload, and, by in effect crashing it on the runway, he put at risk the lives of his crew and of the other bombers taking off behind him.

Dennis Bird (retired squadron leader), Shoreham-by-Sea,
West Sussex

With the exceptions of Queen Victoria, Edith Cavell and Boudicca, are there any public statues of women in London?

Yes, several. The most prominent is probably that of Queen Anne, a marble statue by Richard Belt, in front of St Paul's Cathedral. There's a lead statue of Queen Charlotte in Queen Square, WC1; a bronze one of Queen Alexandra at the London hospital, E1; and a stone one of Elizabeth I over the vestry porch of St Dunstan in the West, EC4. Florence Nightingale stands with her lamp both in Waterloo Place, SW1, and outside St Thomas's hospital, SE1; and a marble Sarah Siddons stands on Paddington Green, W2.

A stone Mary Queen of Scots is in a first-floor niche at 143–4 Fleet Street, and a bronze statue of Mrs William (Catherine) Booth is in Champion Park, SE5. A bronze group in Lincoln's Inn Fields, WC2, shows Margaret MacDonald, the social worker (and Ramsay's wife), holding out her arms to nine little children. Princess Pocahontas reclines in Red Lion Square, WC1. And Emmeline Pankhurst is in Victoria Tower Gardens, SW1.

Chris Birch, London SW6

Had the Duke of Windsor not abdicated and remained King until his death, who would be the sovereign now?

Assuming that he married Mrs Simpson and this union produced no children, as was the case, his eldest surviving brother, Henry, Duke of Gloucester, would have become King Henry IX in 1972 at the age of seventy-two. Henry's reign would have lasted only two years before his death in 1974. Of Henry's two sons, the eldest, William, had died in a tragic accident two years before his father's death, thus leaving his brother, Richard Duke of Gloucester, to ascend to the throne as King Richard IV in 1974 and remain as such to the present day. Having only reached his forty-fifth birthday in 1989, his reign would look set to be one of the longest in our history and certainly more lengthy and agreeable than that of his namesake and only other Duke of Gloucester to reign over us, Richard III.

A. W. Overhead, Wellingborough, Northants

Mr Overhead would, in an earlier time, be in danger of losing his head over the traitorous proposition that an heir to the throne having the misfortune to predecease the sovereign thereby disinherits his own heirs. In 1837 when William IV, the third and eldest surviving son of George III, died childless (or at least without legitimate issue) the crown passed not to the fifth son, Ernest Duke of Cumberland, nor to the sixth son, the Duke of Sussex, nor yet to the seventh son, the Duke of Cambridge, but to the daughter of the predeceased fourth son, the late Duke of Kent. English history would have been very different with King Ernest I instead of Queen Victoria on the throne. In the same way, if Edward VIII had not abdicated but had still died childless in 1972, the crown would have gone to the next eldest brother (George, Duke of York) but as he had already died it would not have gone to the next surviving brother (Henry, Duke of Gloucester) but to the Duke of York's daughter – none other than Elizabeth II.

Your (and Her Majesty's) loyal servant.

Ian Verber, Richmond, North Yorks

Note: our thanks to seventy-six other readers who wrote to make this point.

In response to Mr Verber and the seventy-six other loyalists, I must outline my plan to save my traitorous head. My reference to Richard III was no idle remark. I was actually plotting to gain my own place in history by initiating the second war of the Roses. By reading Anne Mortimer for Elizabeth II and Henry Bolingbroke for Richard Duke of Gloucester, any historians among you will realize my cunning plan. The situation that arose during the fifteenth century was remarkably similar to that which would have arisen had the Duke of Windsor not abdicated. Anne Mortimer was the female descendant of the second son of Edward III, and Henry Bolingbroke was the male descendant of the third son of Edward III. Although Anne had a stronger claim, she and her family were swept aside by the ambitious Henry and the House of Lancaster. Despite Anne's claim being further strength-ened by her marriage to Richard of York (descendant of fourth son of Edward III), her family remained in the shadow of the Lancastrian kings, Henry IV, V and VI, who basked in the glory of the war against France. The House of York then seized their opportunity when Henry VI lapsed into insanity and Anne's son Richard became Lord Protector in 1454. When Henry regained his sanity the following year, the struggle between the two houses broke out into the war of the Roses. So it would appear that my coup has been nipped in the bud – and how disturbing it was to realize that the citizen who thwarted my efforts should reside in the county of Yorks.

A. W. Overhead, Wellingborough, Northants

Everybody knows French is derived from Latin. So what did the Gauls speak before Caesar?

Gaulbedegook.

Steve Oliver, Whitstable, Kent

It is not quite correct to say that French is derived entirely from Latin. As pointed out by Henri Hubert in *The History of The Celtic People*, the French vocabulary is derived from Latin but the grammatical structure is not, because it lacks the Latin inflected case structure. French is a more analytical language with a structure resembling Celtic. Hubert suggests that, during a Roman occupation of about five hundred years, the Gauls gradually absorbed Latin words but used them in their own way, developing a kind of Latinized Celtic. Gaul was then taken over by Germanic Franks who thereby gave their name to the country. They failed to impose their German on the Gauls; instead, they learnt to speak this Latinized Celtic, but with a dreadful

German accent, thus giving rise to what became the French language.

W. S. Robertson, Glasgow

How did fishwives get such a bad press?

Before the invention of condoms, the pill, and education for women, the avenues for women to support themselves other than by marriage were extremely meagre. Marriage was the be-all and end-all of existence, and an early grave from constant childbearing was the outcome. Women were connected with the sale of fish in London from medieval times – it was one way they could avoid marriage and earn money to live. They were permitted to buy fish from fishmongers but not to keep a stall, and had to walk the streets carrying their wares. Billingsgate market was their headquarters and fishwives' 'scolding' (or language) became notorious. 'Billingsgate' was synonymous with foul language, and by the time of the Restoration the term 'fishwife' meant anyone who swore.

Olive Marshall, Market Harborough, Leics

Who decides on what date Easter falls?

The *Book Of Common Prayer* contains the method for determining on what day Easter falls. It involves something called the Golden Number or Prime, which must be calculated for the year in question and is one of the most entertaining parts of the church's writings. I would recommend that everyone of any persuasion read this part of the BCP, and it is a good argument for renaming Easter 'The bank holiday that's usually in April but not always'.

Matthew Payne, London

Is there any reference in authentic Jewish historical records to the massacre of male infants up to two years of age between 8 BC and AD 6?

There is no trace of this story anywhere except for the one reference in Matthew's gospel. The story is not historically impossible. Herod was a ruthless killer who murdered a number of his own children. It would have been entirely in character for him to have acted in this way. Since the number of children involved would have been quite small, the lack of reference to this story in other sources is not of itself decisive.

On the other hand, Matthew, in his stories about the infancy of Jesus, seeks to present the truth about Jesus through what are closer to being meditations on Old Testament texts rather than simple, bald historical statements. Throughout his gospel he seeks to show that Jesus is the new Moses. Here, just as Pharaoh slaughtered the children before the birth of Moses, so now Herod does the same before the birth of Jesus. In both cases, however, God foils the plans of tyrants and proceeds to liberate his people. In probability, therefore, the origin of this story is not history but reflection on an Old Testament text.

(The Rev.) Martin Camroux, Birkenhead, Wirral

The Jewish-Roman historian, Josephus, gives a fascinating, if partisan, account of Herod's career in the Jewish war. Herod is portrayed as a brilliant ruler but a ruthless and brutal man who ordered the execution of his favourite wife, Mariamne, in a fit of jealously. He had no compunction in torturing and murdering anyone he believed was implicated in real or imaginary plots against him. No one was safe – brother, mother-in-law, sisters-in-law, brothers-in-law. It was said that it was safer to be Herod's pig (in view of his conformity to Jewish dietary law) than his son. His two sons by Mariamne were strangled and he ordered the execution of his eldest son and heir only five days before his own death.

Herod was obviously aware of how unpopular he was with his subjects and Josephus describes how he planned one last monstrous outrage. As he lay dying in agony, he locked up the leading men from towns and villages all over Judaea in the hippodrome, with instructions that they were to be butchered as soon as he died. He thus hoped to ensure that there would be weeping and mourning at his death instead of the expected wild rejoicings. Happily, his sister made sure the prisoners were released before they could be murdered. A man as callous as this would not hesitate to massacre a few baby boys in an insignificant little village if he thought one of them might be a threat to him.

Linda Holmes, Cottingham, North Humberside

The story is part of the myth that grew up around the concept of Jesus as the Messiah, the destined King of Israel. A similar slaughter was rumoured to have been carried out by King Arthur, and there are parallels in African traditions. The idea, a very ancient one, is that the old king, hoping to be immortal, goes to any length to prevent the conception, birth and survival of his successor. Behind this, no doubt, is the subterranean enmity of fathers towards the sons who will grow to manhood as they themselves decline towards death.

C. C. Wrigley, Lewes, East Sussex

Assuming that most Saxon, Norman and medieval communities would have required a varied mix of skilled people in order to survive, why are there so many Smiths in relation to Weavers, Coopers,

Bakers and Wrights? And what did Jones do originally?

Smiths were very good at picking chastity belts.

Brendan Cooper, London

Having worked all day on something hot and sweaty, it obviously came naturally to continue at night. I realize that this does not explain the relative lack of Rogers but I shall leave this to others more expert than I.

Maurice Childs, Bromley, Kent

The prevalence of Smiths presumably dates from the many centuries when the only mode of transport was a horse. So every town – however insignificant – would have had its own smithy. Perhaps not everyone had a cart (or the wheel rims didn't wear out so fast); so there were not so many wrights, nor much call for barrel-makers (coopers), bakers or weavers.

As for Jones, this is a shortened form for Johnson – and similar abbreviation applies to Evans, Williams, Hughes, Davis, etc.

Graham R. Jones, Manchester

It is wrong to conclude that there were more smiths than wrights or coopers. Small variations in the frequency of names, which happen by chance, are magnified as the generations pass. I made a computer simulation of a village of 100 couples, with twenty each of Wrights, Smiths, Jones, Coopers and Weavers. I assumed that every couple makes ten attempts to reproduce, and that each attempt has a 1 in ten chance of success. This ensures that the population stays roughly stable. The simulation ran for fifty generations (about a thousand years). I tried it 200 times, and the results varied greatly. Usually one or more names die off altogether, and it is very common for one or two names to become dominant. If we could wind back to 1100 and start again, the dominant name might turn out to be Weaver or any of the others.

Chris Brew, Edinburgh

Smith is from the same root as Smitan which means 'to smite', and is one of the few Old English bynames to be recorded a century before the Norman Conquest.

Smith of the tenth century was a worker in iron, smiting ingots into swords, shields, battle-axes, halberds and ploughshares. But the occupational term 'smith' embraced other workers who smote their raw materials; it lost its precision and new names were needed. They were found in another Old English word, *wryhta*: wright or craftsman, subsequently dividing into Cartwright, Wheelwright and Wainwright (maker of wains or waggons).

With increasing specialization, a distinction had to be made between a worker in iron and a worker in tin, so more exact definitions were made, hence blacksmith and whitesmith.

The smith was an important man in medieval times, making and repairing swords, lances, defensive iron-works for castles and manor houses, offensive engines for assaulting enemy castles, and peaceful items such as agricultural implements. He was the technologist and technician, the engineer and mechanic of his day.

There are several reasons why Smith is such a widespread surname: it is one of the oldest Anglo-Saxon names, so Smiths have been around longer than most. The Smiths of Old England were a strong, lusty, vigorous people capable of raising large families. Because he was not quite so close to the heat of battle in medieval warfare as Archers, Bowman (Bowmen), Knights and others, Smith probably returned safely to his native village after the war, to resume his work and the care of his family.

Kenneth Allen, Cook, Australia

Who was or is the Marquis of Granby and why does he have so many pubs named after him?

John Manners, Marquis of Granby (1721–70), was commander of the British troops who served under Prince Ferdinand of Brunswick in Germany during the Seven Years' War. He was 'a generous, genial character, much loved by his troops and popular with the public' (Savory, *His Britannic Majesty's Army In Germany During The Seven Years' War*). He was prepared to buy supplies out of his own pocket when official sources failed, and died heavily in debt. A brave fighting soldier, his finest hour was probably when he led Ferdinand's heavy cavalry into action at the Battle of Warburg (31 July 1760), his bald head shining in the sun (hence the phrase 'to charge bald-headed').

As for the pubs, it was common to name them after war heroes (Duke of Wellington, Nelson, etc.), though their number in this case seems to have been increased by discharged soldiers who set up pubs named after their old commander.

Michael Bell, London SW16

In the days before pensions for common soldiers or a welfare state, it was established practice for high-ranking officers to buy pubs for men who had served them in some exceptional way. This then acted as a form of pension, and reached a height during and after the Napoleonic War. There was no strict rule as to how or when this honour should be awarded, but the Marquis of Granby was famous for the number of pubs he gave away, and which were named after him in turn. This practice is the main reason for such names in pre-1900 pubs, some of which, such as the Marquis of Lorne in Brixton, south London, may be the only surviving memorial to a lesser (or less generous) leader.

Steve Wilson, London SE2

Michael Bell gave a very good account of John Manners, Marquis of Granby (1721–70), but the man alluded to in so many public house names is his grandson Samuel Manners (1772–1837). Samuel was an antiquarian with a particular fascination for medieval taverns, many of which were being altered or demolished at the time. He had a couple of the better examples dismantled and rebuilt on his Nottinghamshire estate. Fascination eventually turned to obsession and Samuel even had the facade of the thirteenth-century Saracens Head, Northampton, re-erected as the north wall of his bathroom. Many pubs bearing his name have done so in memory of his eccentric passion for public houses, but it is thought that he did pay some landlords to name their pubs after him during his lifetime, notably the original Scruffy Murphy in Leicester.

Reginald Spandit, The Granby Society, Tewkesbury

My father has maintained for years that Billy the Kid was shot and killed, not by Pat Garrett, but by the owner of the house in which he was staying. Is there any evidence to support this theory?

Everyone 'knows' that Pat Garrett killed Billy the Kid in Pete Maxwell's house at old Fort Sumner around midnight on 14 July 1881 – but (to paraphrase John O'Hara on the death of George Gershwin) you don't have to believe it if you don't want to. Conspiracy theory fans have been having fun with the proposition for years. It is generally believed that Billy was staying with Celsa Gutierres, a married woman who had been his mistress. Making her carpenter husband, Sabal, the killer is a wonderful new twist to the story. However, most researchers are fairly satisfied that at the time Kid was killed it was not Celsa who was his sweetheart, but Pablita, Pete Maxwell's teenage sister, who was pregnant with his child and who was hastily married off to one Jose Jaramillo within months of the Kid's death.

So the owner of the house in which he was killed, rather than staying, also had a good motive for wanting the Kid out of the way. But whether those midnight doings at Fort Sumner were indeed any darker than history records, we shall probably never learn, although it would he interesting to know upon what information the questioner's father bases his theory. Other stories abound: my favourite has the Kid discovered in bed with Pablita and shot *in flagrante delicto*, an enviable way to shuffle off this mortal coil.

Frederick Nolan, Chalfont St Giles, Bucks

Why did men of fashion in the eighteenth century wear shoes with scarlet heels? Was it a mark of rank?

Low-cut shoes, with high heels in a different colour from that of the shoe, became fashionable in the late seventeenth century at the court of Louis XIV, no doubt reflecting the king's taste. The most popular colour was red, which was also a popular colour for silk stockings at that time. This fashion spread to other countries and lasted well into the eighteenth century. In England they went out of fashion in the middle of the eighteenth century, but were revived briefly by Charles James Fox, the Whig statesman, in 1770.

Patsy Conway, Tring, Herts

When was the last man 'pressed' into the Royal Navy?

The navy last used impressment during the War of 1812, fought between Britain and the US. Indeed, the practice was substantially the cause – ships of the Royal Navy having been press-ganging British-born seamen from American vessels to fight against the French. Shortly before the American declaration of war, the patrol vessel *Musquito* was found to be shorthanded, and intercepted a group of lobster boats off the German island of Heligoland, forcibly impressing Samuel Payne, an experienced fisherman, and John Thorogood, an apprentice. The men's colleagues sued for their release, and were granted a writ of habeas corpus, arguing that the Heligoland fisheries, possessed by the British since 1807, fell within a defined statutory exception. This incident illustrates how impressment differs from formal conscription into national service, being ad hoc, arbitrary and (unless challenged in court) entirely undocumented.

When, forty years later, the navy next fought a major war, in the Crimea, the decision was made to proceed without impressment – and the success of this policy resulted in the practice falling into abeyance. However, the power (in occasions of need) to impress into the Navy any person of a seafaring character – excluding ferrymen and 'gentlemen' – remains within the royal prerogative; although the royal warrant to the naval authorities does not currently permit this power to be exercised.

Tom Hennell, Withington, Cheshire

Is there anyone in Britain under the age of fifty who uses the first-name Reginald?

My father is Reginald Walker (seventy-five years), my husband is Reginald Price (fifty-one) and my twelve-year-old son is Reginald Price (the third). The youngest does actually prefer to be called Regi.

Lesley Price, Guildford, Surrey

In the years 1930–50, every cinema worthy of the name had a theatre organ, invariably played by a gentleman called Reginald, whose name would be plastered all over the building. With the demise of the instrument, the organists slipped into obscurity, and newly born infants were christened Peregrine, Goldolphin or Joe.

William Watson, Liverpool

The questioner would be in fine company here in Papua New Guinea. Here in Dogura there is Reginald Tereakina (aged forty-two), the post master, and Reginald Mine (twelve), from Agaun, who attends the school. Say what you like about the missionary history here, but it has left some good solid names. The school also boasts three Agneses, two Ethels, two Ednas, three Arthurs and two Alfreds.

On the name scene, there are some other oddities nearby: Adolf Hitler Moduladula (twelve) lives in Topura, Gary Linikar (ten) in Gadovisu and Elvis Prasley is alive and well and tending his fields up in Boyaboya.

Ed Griffin, Dogura, Papua New Guinea

In the early eighties I worked as a midwifery tutor in Dogura, Papua New Guinea, from where Ed Griffin replied. I remember one morning particularly well: supervising Cinderella in the path lab, being introduced to Francis of Assissi on the outpatients' verandah and then having a surprise meeting with George Washington in the radio room!

Cynthia McVey, Newtown, Powys

When Shelley drowned in a boating accident, his wife Mary and Lord Byron burnt his body on a funeral pyre. Mary rescued his heart from the flames and kept it in a casket for the rest of her life. What happened to the heart?

Shelley's cremation, stage-managed by his friend of only six months, Trelawny, was attended by Trelawny himself, Lord Byron, Leigh Hunt, who had travelled to Italy to join Shelley and Byron in a publishing venture, and various local officers. Mary did not attend and, according to Trelawny's account, the others could hardly face it; Byron swimming off to his boat and Hunt remaining in his carriage. Trelawny observed that Shelley's heart was not consumed in the fire and rescued it, burning his hand and risking quarantine in the process.

Hunt lay claim to it from Trelawny, justifying his action to Mary, who assumed a natural right to possession in a letter: '. . . for [Hunt's love of Shelley] to make way for the claims of any other love, man's or woman's, I must have great reasons indeed brought to me . . . In his case above all other human beings, no ordinary appearance of rights, not even yours, can affect me.'

Byron was asked to intervene but flippantly questioned Hunt's need for the heart ('He'll only . . . write sonnets on it'), and it was through the efforts of Jane Williams, the Shelleys' friend, whose partner Edward had drowned with Shelley, that Hunt was eventually persuaded to part with the relic and Mary took charge of it.

At Mary Shelley's death in 1851, the heart was found in her desk wrapped in a copy of Adonais, Shelley's self-prophesying eulogy on the death of Keats. It was kept in a shrine with other relics at Boscombe Manor, the home of Shelley's son, and finally buried in 1889 in the family vault in Bournemouth.

Abbie Mason, Cambridge

Amy Wallace, in the second *Book Of Lists*, writes:

There is a peculiar note of irony to the whole affair. The organ that longest survives a fire is not the heart but the liver – and no one present at Shelley's funeral knew enough about anatomy to tell the difference. This theory would explain the legend that the heart was unusually large.

David Cottis, London SW15

A more precise location of Shelley's heart is the graveyard of Peter's church, Bournemouth, where it shares a resting place with the remains of other such worthies as Mary Wollstonecraft, eighteenth-century feminist, and Sir Dan Godfrey, founder in 1893 of the precursor of the Bournemouth Symphony Orchestra.

John Gritten, London

No one interested in Shelley's heart should omit to read Timothy Webb's 'Religion Of The Heart' (*Keats–Shelley Review*, Autumn 1992). The reader will learn that Shelley's heart was not unusually large, but unusually small — according to Trelawny, who snatched it from the fire. It was Hunt who changed Trelawny's account probably, as Webb plausibly argued, because he could not face the idea of a Shelley with a diminished organ of benevolence.

Hunt himself was well equipped to know the heart from the liver, having been much struck when young by some preserved hearts among the anatomical specimens of a Lincolnshire surgeon. So we must look for an explanation, other than anatomical confusion, for why Shelley's heart would not burn. A condition leading to progressive calcification is one possibility that has been advanced. The irony of the whole affair might well be that Shelley's heart was becoming literally, though not metaphorically, a heart of stone.

Nora Crook, Cambridge

According to John Gritten, Mary Wollstonecraft is buried in Bournemouth. But while her body may be there, her memorial headstone is still in London's Old St Pancras churchyard, behind the station.

Paul S. Coates, University Of East London

Who first lay back and thought of England?

Alice, Lady Hillingdon, in her journal, 1912:

> I am happy now that Charles calls on my bedchamber less frequently than of old. As it is, I now endure but two calls a week and when I hear his steps outside my door I lie down on my bed, close my eyes, open my legs and think of England.

N. G. Macbeth, Kenilworth

FAMOUS PEOPLE

Has anyone, famous or otherwise, ever successfully faked their own death?

Elvis, surely?

Matthew Scudamore, London

Who is Norbert Dentressangle, and why does he own so many red trucks?

According to a 1993 article in *France* magazine, Norbert Dentressangle is a Frenchman, then aged around forty and living in St-Vallier, between Valence and Lyon, with his wife and two children. He owns one of Europe's most successful freight-forwarding companies with depots all across Europe (hence the red trucks). Along with a British

125

company, Eddie Stobart, Norbert's trucks are the object of a cult following.

Ian Rice, Stockport

I'm afraid your correspondent Ian Rice has fallen into Norbert's trap. My family and I have watched his expansion with growing concern and it seems clear to us that he is carrying out detailed reconnaissance for a coup when he deems the time to be ripe. What we have not yet discovered are his training grounds nor whether Eddie Stobart is an ally or a rival; can anyone help?

Julian Loring, Downton, Salisbury

Whenever the 'I thought he was dead' conversation arises, a friend and I always muse about the 'deadest' well-known rock group. We think it is Canned Heat, who have only two of the classic line-up still alive. Are there any completely dead rock groups? Which is the deadest rock group?

The Grateful Dead have lost four members, including leader Jerry Garcia (1995, heart attack). There have been serious problems keeping the keyboard slot filled: the group lost their founding ivory tinkler, Ron (Pigpen) McKernan (1973, liver failure), then it was Keith Godchaux (1980, car accident) and Brent Mydland (1990, overdose). Lately, pianist Bruce Hornsby has tempted fate by touring with the group.

Motorcycles are the bane of the Allman Brothers Band. Crashes killed singer-guitarist Duane Allman in 1971 and bassist Berry Oakley a year later. Oakley's replacement Lamar Williams (1983, cancer) managed to live a few years after leaving them.

The New York Dolls have paid a hefty price for their indulgences. Among the casualties are founding drummer Bill Murcia (1972, overdose), guitarist Johnny Thunders (1991, overdose), replacement drummer Jerry Nolan (1992, stroke) and bassist Arthur Kane (2004, leukaemia). Even though David Johansen and Syl Sylvain are the Dolls' only surviving members, they still tour with a backing band.

Lynyrd Skynyrd suffered their first tragedy in 1977 – an aeroplane crash that killed singer Ronnie van Zant, guitarist Steve Gaines and his sister, back-up singer Cassie Gaines. Though Van Zant and guitarist Allen Collins originally wrote 'Free Bird' as a tribute to Duane Allman, the song morphed into a memorial for the fallen trio. Collins himself is now gone (1990, respiratory failure). He was followed by bassist Leon Wilkeson (2001, liver failure).

The Ramones, having spearheaded the punk movement, called it quits in the late nineties. Without the band, Joey (2001, lymphatic cancer), Dee Dee (2002, heroin overdose) and Johnny (2004, prostate cancer) followed suit. Tommy Ramone, the last founding member, left the band in 1977. He's had a successful career as a producer.

But the deadliest job in rock has to be the drummer for Spinal Tap. Legend has it that a series of bizarre gardening accidents and unfortunate explosions has claimed no fewer than six of the mythical band's drummers – Joe (Mama) Besser, Peter (James) Bond, Eric (Stumpy Joe) Childs, John (Stumpy) Pepys and brothers Mick and Ric Shrimpton.

Andrew Muir, Shrewsbury

Tyrannosaurus/T-Rex have lost founder Marc Bolan (car crash, 1977), second percussionist Mickey Finn (natural causes, 2003), T-Rex original bassist Steve Currie (car crash, 1981), original percussionist Steve Peregrin Took (cocktail cherry, 1980), leaving no one alive from Tyrannosaurus Rex and only Bill Legend (drummer) from the first full T-Rex line-up, although the rest of the final line-up survive, including Marc's wife Gloria Jones.

Steve Wilson, London E6

The Temptations' classic hit line-up of 1964–7 has only one surviving member from the original five, Otis Williams, who still leads a version of the group to this day. But judged purely on appearance, the Stones take some beating.

Kingsley Abbott, Diss, Norfolk

After unseating Nilsson's 'Without You', they spent five weeks at the top of the British charts in spring 1972 with a 'heavy' version of 'Amazing Grace', before being knocked off themselves by T-Rex with 'Metal Guru'. I am referring, of course, to The Pipes and Drums and Military Band of the Royal Scots Dragoon Guards, formed in 1689 – and with not a solitary original member or any of the immediate replacements left alive.

Alan Clayson, Henley, Oxon

Who is/was the most stupid person ever born?

A lot of people will probably put George W. as the answer to this question, but I think he's misunderestimated.

Tim Campbell, Wigan

The retiring American senator, Fritz Hollings, recently said that George W. Bush was the worst White House resident in fifty years. Is he the worst American president in history?

Far from it. Most historians point to Warren G. Harding, who presided over the most corrupt administration in American history and was (supposedly) poisoned by his wife because of his infidelities. I'm a Republican and

we've been quietly disowning the creep for decades.
Michael del Valle, Detroit, US

I think it's a tie between G. W. Bush and R. M. Nixon.
A. Wells, US

Don McLean wrote the song 'American Pie' as a tribute to Buddy Holly. The lyrics are enigmatic and seem loaded with allusions. What do they mean?

As with many other allusive pieces of writing, like 'The Waste Land', the effect is more to do with the creation of atmosphere, evoking several images at the same time, than a simple 'a-means-b' relationship. However, a few things can be said with assurance. The most important thing to remember is that the song isn't simply about the death of Buddy Holly, although that is certainly the theme of the first verse. After that, the song offers a chronological account of American youth throughout the sixties, focusing on the later years of that decade. There are several references to specific individuals, some more obvious than others. So, for instance, the Jester is Bob Dylan, the line 'with the Jester on the sidelines in a cast' a reference to the motorcycle accident that temporarily halted his career. The King is Elvis Presley (of course), the Queen I'm not sure about. The Quartet are the Beatles, hence the previous line's 'while Lenin read a book on Marx' (McLean pronounces Lenin as 'Lennon') and the park is Candlestick Park, San Francisco, where they played their last live concert (another 'day the music died.') Jack Flash, unsurprisingly, is Mick Jagger, as is the 'Satan' (an allusion to the Stones' 'Sympathy for the Devil') later on in the verse, which seems to deal with the Altamont concert, where the group's Hell's Angel bodyguards (hence 'no angel born in hell/Could break that Satan's spell') stabbed to death a young black concertgoer named Meredith Hunter. 'A girl who sang the blues' is Janis Joplin, and 'The Father, Son and Holy Ghost' refers both to the three singers who died on Buddy Holly's plane (Holly himself, Richie Valens and J. P. Richardson, the Big Bopper) and to the three most prominent assassination victims of the sixties, Martin Luther King, Bobby Kennedy and J. F. K.

The song's non-musical allusions are rather less straightforward. However, I would say that it alludes to events including the Charles Manson killings ('Helter Skelter/In a summer swelter': the Beatles' 'Helter Skelter' was the song that 'inspired' Manson's family), the Vietnam war ('the Sergeants played a marching tune' – a reference to Sergeant Barry Sadler's gung-ho 'Ballad of the Green Beret'), anti-war demonstrations, including the 1968 riots at the Democrats' Chicago convention ('The players tried to take the field/The marching band refused to yield'), and Woodstock ('there we were all in one place'). Overall then, 'American Pie' paints a picture of the sixties, linked by a number of 'days the music died', from Buddy Holly's death, the singer's teenage romance, Candlestick Park, Chicago 1968 and Altamont through to the decade's uncertain end. It's one of the first songs to deal with the death of sixties optimism, and one of the most effective.

David Cottis, Cardiff

The name of the programme escapes me, but the conversation followed these lines: Interviewer: 'Don, the song has been a bestseller for years and is now studied in university courses, so what does it really mean?' Don: 'It means that I don't have to work unless I want to.'

Gus Stewart, London W7

Was Mrs Thatcher evil?

Yes. (I thought these were supposed to be questions that were difficult to answer.)

Daniel Owen, London

No. She led a government that had to do what it did – and in many respects, did not go far enough – and was supported by the British people for that reason. As a consequence she is hated by many leftwing people who prefer easy illusions to hard realities.

Alex Swanson, Milton Keynes

If she is, then the British people (myself included) have only themselves to blame. We voted her in three times. Evil doesn't really manifest itself in democratically elected politicians – if it did, she wouldn't have won a second election, but she did. The joke, I'm afraid, is on us.

Graeme Deacon, Wellington, New Zealand

Margaret Thatcher was beautiful, caring, strong, creative and the most excellent politician of the twentieth century. We should thank God for her.

Baz Ganley, Swadlincote, Derbys

Come on Baz. Let's look at these marvellous characteristics embodied by your wonderful Mrs T. The poll tax was certainly creative. She showed her caring side to the miners, and the Belgrano incident, I thought, displayed real strength of character. And as for beautiful? What a hottie.

As for all this stuff about 'us' electing her – you might have. I certainly never did.

Seth Chanas, Edinburgh

To answer Seth, 'we' did vote her in. His vote, if cast, was taken into account, even if not in favour. Individuals cannot opt out of democratic decisions just because they dislike the result.

To use the term evil to describe a courageous politician debases both debate and language. I agree she did what was necessary to change Britain. As a student in the seventies, life and the future looked dull and grey. Then from 1979 onwards anything was possible, including making a successful economy that could afford to spend its surplus on others, nationally and internationally. If 'we' didn't do this, it is again the fault of democracy, not Margaret Thatcher.

Ian Whitehouse, London

She scores five out of five on the definitions in my dictionary: 1. Morally bad or wrong; 2. Causing ruin, injury, or pain; harmful: the evil effects of a poor diet; 3. Characterized by or indicating future misfortune; ominous: evil omens. 4. Bad or blameworthy by report; infamous: an evil reputation; 5. Characterized by anger or spite; malicious: an evil temper.

Justin Rigden, Adelaide, Australia

I have a theory that George Orwell's *Nineteen Eighty-Four* is the most referenced book in modern culture. Is there anyway to find out whether this is true?

You could ask the Ministry of Truth.

David Morton, Nottingham

Mother Goose is celebrated in pantomime, and is recorded as having been buried at St Olave's church, London EC3, on 14 September 1586. But who was she?

There is a legend that this pantomime/nursery rhyme character was based on an actual woman from Boston, US, named Elizabeth Goose (sometimes 'Vergoose' or 'Vertigoose') who is supposed to have written a book of children's rhymes in 1719. Elizabeth Goose's grave certainly exists, but there is no evidence that she did write such a book.

The character Mother Goose was first associated with nursery rhymes in a book published by John Newberry & Co in 1781 entitled *Mother Goose's Melody Or Sonnets From The Cradle*. The oldest extant copy dates from 1791, but it is thought that an edition appeared as early as 1765. Newbury appears to have derived the name 'Mother Goose' from a collection of fairy tales published in 1697 by the French author Charles Perrault, entitled *Contes De Ma Mère l'Oye*. This translates as 'Tales of my Mother Goose', a French folk expression roughly equivalent to the English 'old wives' tales'.

Nick Spokes, Ilford, Essex

Can a person like Wagner's music and still be a socialist?

The Perfect Wagnerite, George Bernard Shaw's book, argues that Wagner's *Ring* cycle is a political allegory offering a critique of capitalism. For Shaw, the Gods are to be interpreted as the aristocracy, the Giants as peasants, the Nibelungs as the proletariat and Alberich as a capitalist. Even Siegfried, the sword-wielding superman himself, is a model for a free socialist New Man, destined to destroy this oppressive system. Unfortunately, Shaw says, Wagner comes over all soppy at the crucial moment and the allegory collapses into a lot of gush about redemption through love.

Nevertheless the *Ring* gives us some idea of what a future socialist art might be like. This may seem odd given Wagner's later association with nazism, but it must be remembered that at this time socialist and fascist ideas actually overlapped in many areas. Wagner had some pretty unpleasant opinions, mainly in his later years, but he also believed in the prospect of an art that would recapture the relationship between popular appeal and cultural sophistication that had existed in Shakespeare's day. He wanted the widest possible audience to be in touch with the musical inheritance of Beethoven and with the power of drama that combined the achievements of Sophocles and Shakespeare. In these days of postmodern cultural fragmentation and consumer culture, that's not a bad vision of a truly socialist art.

Julie Byrne, Liverpool

If Wagner is suspect, where does that leave Chopin (a virulent anti-Semite), Puccini (an honorary member of the Italian Fascist party) and Stravinsky (who revered Mussolini)? As D. H. Lawrence said: 'Don't judge the artist, trust the tale.'

Jonathan Yglesias, London N10

Did Adam and Eve have navels?

In Genesis 1:26, God (displaying his own disconcerting tendency to plurality) says: 'Let us make man in our own image, and let them have dominion over the fish of the sea.' So 'man' was a collective being from the beginning.

As for Adam and Eve, the names occur much later on in the text, after the Fall, and mean something like 'red' or 'earthy' and 'living' or 'lively'. So they're symbolic qualities, and were presumably consciously attached to symbolic persons. It took a later, less-aware culture to start treating these allusive stories as literal histories.

So the first humanity wasn't very different from present-day humanity, belly buttons and all, and the power of creation stories can still be recaptured by those who gaze beyond their own navels.

David Newton, Chelmondiston, Suffolk

'Yes' is the short answer. It could be argued that the Adam created in God's own image was navel-less: sexual reproduction only came on to the scene after the expulsion from Eden, and the navel is a mark of our fallen state.

In the last century a creationist rearguard action against Darwinism centred on Adam's navel. Philip Gosse's book *Omphalos* (Greek: navel) argued that, although Adam was created, his body looked as if he had once been born; similarly, although the animals in the Garden of Eden were created as adults, they looked as if they had been born and grown in the normal way. Gosse's masterstroke was to extend the argument to the earth itself, which 'appeared' as if it dated back millions of years. However, neither creationists nor evolutionists were impressed with this, and the case for a scientifically respectable creationism duly perished.

Phil Edwards, Manchester

My theory is that when God had finished making man he realized that Adam just didn't look right with that expanse of smooth, featureless abdomen, so he created the belly button. Later, when placentation became just the thing, it was the perfect place for the umbilical cord to attach to the foetus.

(Dr) Kitty Smith, London N8

Is there any evidence to support the theory that the bandleader Glenn Miller did not die in a plane crash but was in fact murdered in the Pigalle district of Paris and that the truth was hidden by the authorities for reasons of wartime morale?

At the time of Glenn Miller's disappearance I was a radar operator on the east coast. I can remember going on watch when Filter Room was querying plots on a VIP track that appeared to be deviating from its expected course. The following day we heard the VIP had been Glenn Miller. I believe he was alone. There was a rumour that he was trying to get back to America and didn't make it.

Dorothy Carter, Buchie, Banffshire

The flight that Glenn Miller reputedly took was not a scheduled flight. My father, E. F. Woods, was a communications engineer, serving in Eisenhower's staff operating from Brussels. He and his team were scheduled to fly back to the UK when the flight was requisitioned by the Glenn Miller Band. The plane of course vanished. After the war he made several attempts to get his story published and the 'fictional' story corrected. The attempts failed. He, and the others concerned, were certain there was a mystery and I would be very interested to hear of any more clues.

(Dr) Mike Woods, Bradford

Miller was flying to the continent, not from it. In fact, to Paris and not from Brussels to England. There were no scheduled flights in 1944. The aircraft was a single-engined Norseman carrying Miller, an Army Air Corps colonel and the pilot. The weather on Friday 15 December 1944 was bad with poor visibility. Miller was advised not to make the flight. No radio communication took place, so the reasons for crashing are not explained; mechanical failure or the weather are the most likely.

Neale Johnson, Essendine, near Stamford, Lincs

'She'll be coming round the mountain when she comes,' promises the old song. Who was she? Which mountain? Did she ever arrive?

According to Carl Sandburg's collection, *The American Songbag* (1927, p373), before the song was altered by 'mountaineers' and then taken over by railroad gangs, it was an African-American spiritual, 'When The Chariot Comes'.

She (the chariot) would be driven by King Jesus, would

be loaded with bright angels, would neither rock nor totter, would run so level and steady, and would take us to the portals. The song virtually invites itself to be adapted to railroads, though the chariot gets lost in the transposition and leaves us with a presumably animate, mysterious 'She'.

Will Kelley, Chicago, US

Who was the man who struck the gong for J. Arthur Rank?

I have never had it verified but, as a young lad, I always understood from an elderly relative that J. Arthur's gong-bonger was Jerome K. Jerome, the author of *Three Men in a Boat*. I have a sneaking feeling that this may not be true; perhaps someone can put my mind at rest.

Michael Manning, Chessington, Surrey

The trademark of a muscle-bound man banging a gong at the beginning of every Rank film was dreamed up in the thirties by the publicity manageress of General Film Distributors, which then distributed J. Arthur's films. The lady had in mind Bombadier Billy Wells, 'Beautiful Billy' to his fans, who had been British heavyweight boxing champion from 1911–19. He was filmed at Walton Hall Studios, Isleworth, in 1935. After the war, it was deemed that Wells should be replaced and his successor was hunky Phil Nieman, who was immortalized at Gainsborough Studios, Shepherd's Bush. Nieman's replacement, in 1955, was yet another athlete, Ken Richmond, who won a wrestling bronze in the 1952 Helsinki Olympics. Richmond, filmed at Pinewood, remains to this day.

Quentin Falk, Little Marlow, Bucks

Who was Gordon Bennett?

James Gordon Bennett (1841–1918) was an American journalist, editor of the *New York Herald* (in succession to his less well-known father, also James Gordon Bennett) and sports enthusiast. He is probably best known now for being the man who commissioned Henry Morton Stanley to search for Dr Livingstone (thus presumably occasioning a telegram that began: 'Gordon Bennett – I've found Livingstone!').

Bennett also introduced polo to the US and was involved in horse racing (Leopold Bloom spends some time in *Ulysses* contemplating a bet upon a horse in the Gordon Bennett Handicap, actually run that day in Dublin).

Nicholas Graham, Teddington, Middx

In January 1876, Stanley saw a great mountain 'afar off' and named it Mount Gordon Bennett. This was later changed to the Ruwenzori, better known, perhaps, as the Mountains of the Moon.

Rennie Bere, Bude, Cornwall

In 1900, he donated the Gordon Bennett Trophy for a race between national teams of drivers and cars. The complex qualifying process for entry led to the exclamation: Gordon Bennett!

George Hartshorn, Badby, Daventry

My sister-in-law, a born-and-bred Eastender, insists that 'Gordon Bennett' is just a politely extended form of 'Gawd', to avoid accusations of blasphemy.

Si Cowe, Pickering, North Yorks

Who was Kilroy when he was here?

'Kilroy was here' is graffiti from the Second World War. James Kilroy was the senior shipyard inspector at the US forces shipping depot at Quincy, Massachusetts, being required to sign for all equipment consigned to ETO (European Theatre of Operations). GIs, finding his name on nearly everything they used, started scrawling the phrase wherever they were based. It then spread around the world with the movement of US forces.

Bernard Goodman, London SE1

According to an article by an American journalist, Susan Ulbing, he was an infantry soldier who got tired of hearing the air force brag that it was always first on the spot. Kilroy specialized in being the first and only one to show up in outrageous places, like the bathroom reserved for Truman, Stalin and Attlee at the Potsdam Conference.

John Idorn, London W8

Who was the first man to do what a man's gotta do, when did he do it and what was it when he'd done it?

The words are often wrongly attributed to John Wayne. They were, in fact, uttered by Shane (Alan Ladd) in the film of the same name. What Shane has to do, in the conscious sense, is kill Wilson (Jack Palance) *et al.*, and pave the way for a peaceful existence for his friends, the homesteaders.

However, there is an undercurrent, touched on in the movie but camouflaged by the superb action scenes and atmospheric location. It is more fully developed in the novel, *Shane*, by Jack Schaeffer, which shows that Shane is obviously in love with his friend's wife (Jean Arthur). There is also a hint that she may be falling in love with Shane while retaining her love for her husband, Joe (Van Heflin). Therefore, Shane must do two things for his friends: he must rid the range of villains, at the cost of his life perhaps; and he must take himself out of their lives for ever. This is what a man has to do, and do it he does.

R. A. Southern, Wigan, Lancs

I don't think your correspondent is quite right in attributing the phrase to Alan Ladd in *Shane*. He uses similar expressions like 'A man has to be what he is' and 'I couldn't do what I gotta do', but never the exact words. The expression does occur in John Steinbeck's *Grapes of Wrath* in chapter 18 (p206 of the Penguin edition) when Casy says 'I know this – a man got to do what he got to do.' This was published in 1939, which predates Shane anyway.

Stephen Collins, Ripon, Yorks

What level of importance must a person have before they are considered a victim of assassination rather than murder?

I would have thought it was down to any impersonal professional/political motive. The act of assassination is surely always about changing a wider circumstance by the death rather than the taking of a private individual's life.

Christopher Preston, Preston, Lancs

But John Lennon is usually described as having been assassinated – does he fulfil the above criteria?

Steven Jackson, Taichuing, Taiwan

I think people use the word 'assassination' in relation to John Lennon because he is seen as a political figure in some way. Many conspiracy theorists still think his murder was a plot by the FBI because they disapproved of his anti-establishment leanings. Or it could just be that they didn't want him to make another album as bad as '*Double Fantasy*'?

Mark Fletcher, London

How did Action Man get that scar on his face?

Plastic surgery.

Liam Welsby, Accrington, Lancs

Action Man's designers wanted to patent the figure – GI Joe in the US. But lawyers advised them that there was little chance of patenting the human body, so they added the scar and were then able to patent it.

Alan Lloyd Schaumburg, Illinois, US

Ken caught him canoodling with Barbie.

Feargal McKay, Dublin

FICTIONAL PEOPLE

Bond kills. Bond drinks. Bond screws. Bond keeps the British end up. Bond achieves all of this and more, although I can't remember him eating very much. Which movies has 007 eaten in?

Not only has Bond eaten, he also discovered a double agent while eating. While on the Orient Express in *From Russia with Love*, Bond shares dinner with Red Grant. When Red Grant turns out to be a member of Spectre, Sean Connery delivers the wonderful line, 'Red wine with fish. Well, that should have told me something.'

Joseph Thomas, London

If the castaways on the island in *Lord of the Flies* had been all girls, would the outcome have been different?

The novel ends with the island on fire, two boys killed and the rest of the tribe more or less insane. The novel charts the struggle for a definitive way to live – whether to live wildly and passionately for the moment, or whether to get back to the Home Counties, and the adult life. The conflict between these two ideologies generates a territorial battle. Young girls can also be frighteningly territorial, particularly over other girls. The leaders of the group would be the older ones, or even those who looked oldest – in other words, those on the onset of puberty. The younger girls would have felt inferior, bewildered, and probably turned on one another in frustration at being left out. Even if there were a few older girls who remembered their manners and were nice to the littl'uns, and tried to maintain domestic bliss, they would eventually become strangely mad too: withered by their desire to be mothers, yet unable to become pregnant. The bad girls, the mad girls, the ones who thought that sisterhood was a cheesy restrictive joke, would run amok, shouting and laughing and battering anyone who attempted to protest. We did this at school – not the battering exactly, but if I'd had a spear, who knows?

Nicola Skinner, Berkhamsted, Herts

Each time I have taught this book for O level/GCSE, I have asked my pupils to rewrite a chosen episode with female characters. To some extent, each new version depends upon the author's gender, but invariably a good deal more attention is lavished on the littl'uns. There's never any nudity – in the first scene on the beach, Rachael always makes a point of keeping her pants on. There is usually a fat, bespectacled girl called Peggy who is teased and derided, but nonetheless keeps her feet firmly on the ground and provides both sound advice and an awareness of the problems they will face.

When Rachael says that her father is a man of influence and will be organizing a rescue party, it is Peggy who says: 'I hope they remember to bring the Tampax Lady.' Jackie, leader of the netball squad, wishes to have an area of the beach permanently reserved for team practice, despite the fact that they don't actually have a ball.

Nobody gets killed, but some suffer acute misery as a result of being excluded from all of the tight and mutually disdainful cliques into which the girls usually divide (each with its own spokesbitch, in one particular bitter and girl-authored version). There is also a tendency for twins, Emma 'n' Erica, to develop distinct personalities and take up a larger share of the plot. In fact, someone really ought to publish Lady of the Spiders – it would make quite an entertaining examination text.

Nevertheless, requiring the revised cast to be mixed rather than single sex tends to provide a significantly greater challenge, and provokes more searching questions on character and motive. In this context, Samantha and Eric definitely come into their own.

Bryn Williams, Navenby, Lincoln

Lord of the Flies is a work informed by theology, not by realism. It dramatizes the Christian belief that people are born 'fallen' in a state of original sin, and in need of redemption. This has now translated into the establishment belief that ordinary human beings need to be overseen by authority or they will tear each other to pieces. No wonder the book is so popular with teachers!

In real life of course, parties of children have been shipwrecked together, over the thousands of years human beings have been travelling by water, and it never ends up with them slaughtering each other and burning the island. I read about some Malaysian boys out fishing who were shipwrecked for several weeks, and survived quite amicably.

I think the only examples where shipwrecked people start to fight each other are where there is an added external stress, such as no food. In the absence of such stresses, boys or girls could manage to get by without adult intervention, if they were old enough to care for their physical needs.

Alison Page, Coventry

In 'Ode To Billy Joe', by Bobbie Gentry, what is it that Billy Joe and his girlfriend throw off the Tallahatchee bridge?

When 'Ode To Billy Joe' was first released, the common belief was that Billy Joe McAllister and his girl threw their newborn baby off the Tallahatchee bridge. However, according to the 1976 film inspired by the song, what Billy Joe and his girlfriend really threw into the river was a rag doll. (The doll, incidentally, had been the subject of another Bobbie Gentry song, 'Benjamin', which appeared on one of her albums.) In the film, the action symbolizes the passage of boy and girl into adulthood, discarding childish ways.

The film, which was scripted with Gentry's blessing, also resolved the mystery of just why Billy Joe jumped off the bridge at all: he couldn't come to terms with a gay encounter he had had with the sawmill owner who employed him. In the final scene, the Bobbie Gentry character leaves town because her family mistakenly assumes she is having Billy Joe's child: pretending to have it is her way of keeping his heroic image alive.

Stephen Barnard, Hatfield, Herts

Boxes full of that dreadful Bobbie Gentry record.

James Canvin, Leicester

Why, when he has superhuman strength and other unearthly powers, does Superman have to be built like a brick outhouse? Surely his feats would be more impressive if he had the build of a 9-stone weakling, into whose face people would generally kick sand?

When originally created, Superman came from a race of super-athletic Adonises on Krypton but wasn't drawn particularly huge – more like a stocky circus strongman. As other superheroes were introduced, Superman's powers increased and multiplied in order to keep him ahead of the pack. Within a few years he had developed into the powerhouse that we all know.

In the eighties, publishers DC Comics tweaked Superman's history: he was rocketed to Earth as a baby but bore no powers when he first arrived. His body acts as a solar battery and it is the sun's energy that powers him. Growing up as a teen on a working farm in Smallville, Kansas, Clark Kent developed a huge physique as a result of his physical labour until his powers emerged at a later date.

The TV show *Smallville* is now also following this concept of Superman's powers developing through his teen years instead of emerging as soon as he arrives on Earth.

Nigel Lowrey, High Wycombe, Bucks

Superman illustrates the phenomenon of independent parallel evolution, but in a slightly different environment. Just as the eye has evolved independently in several terrestrial species, so the intelligent biped mammal has emerged on various planets.

It is evident, however, that the Kryptonian mass was greater than that of the Earth, and the gravitational field correspondingly stronger. To withstand this, Superman and his kind required more powerful bodies than we Earthlings (hence the build). Of course the Kryptonian atmosphere was therefore probably denser, but because the proportion of oxygen in its atmosphere was lower, the result was an oxygen-partial pressure similar to Earth's. This explains Superman's ability to breathe normally.

What we take to be Superman's ability to fly is simply the consequence of a body that evolved in this more powerful gravitational field: to moon dwellers, the 'giant leap' for mankind must have seemed like flight.

Given the biodata we possess on Superman, or can infer, it should be possible to calculate the mass, volume and atmospheric density of Krypton, now that more direct measurements are sadly no longer possible. Any additional information from Miss Lane might allow considerable refinement of the analysis.

Roger Hallam, London N13

Superman is built like a brick outhouse because in the

world of Lycra-clad heroes brawn is associated with goodness, as are good looks though not brains (The Man of Steel is common-sensical rather than brainy).

Correspondingly, intellect is associated with evil. Thus, Superman's foes are brainy as opposed to brawny: Lex Luthor is a plump, bald schemer; Mr Mxyzptlk an impish, grey-haired prankster; Braniac a giant brain housed in a frog-green alien body. And the same applies for other superheroes and their enemies: Batman and The Joker; Spider-Man and The Green Goblin; etc.

Miles Fielder, Edinburgh

In many respects, the *Smallville* TV show has already turned Superman into a less physically imposing character. Until the recent production of *Superman Returns*, Time Warner (owner of DC Comics) had struggled to cash in on the recent superhero movies bandwagon precisely because Superman is popularly perceived as unproblematically invulnerable. At 6 ft 2 in, the recently cast Brandon Routh is 2 in shorter than Christopher Reeve and an inch shorter than Tom Welling, and is athletic rather than muscle-bound.

There has been a shift in superhero adaptations from actors that could physically portray superheroes but arguably lacked a certain psychological nuance or irony – such as Dolph Lundgren in *The Punisher* (1989) and Sylvester Stallone in *Judge Dredd* (1995) – to actors who can more appropriately convey the characters and complexities of modern comic book superheroes while not strictly reflecting their size or physicality, such as Hugh Jackman as Wolverine.

Lorcan McGrane, Norwich, Norfolk

In the Jerome K. Jerome novel *Two Men On The Bummel*, a reference is made to Tom and Jerryism. Since this predates the cartoon characters, who are or were Tom and Jerry?

Tom and Jerry were characters created by Pierce Egan (1772–1849) in his *Life In London; Or The Day And Night Scenes Of Jerry Hawthorne And His Elegant Friend Corinthian Tom, Accompanied By Bob Logic* (1820–1). This was a racy account of the drunken, rowdy behaviour of young Regency bucks. The sequel, *Finish To The Adventures Of Tom, Jerry And Logic* (1828), presented the names in the now-familiar order. This gave rise to the terms 'Tom-and-Jerrying' (1828) and 'Tom-and-Jerryism' (1852) for loutish drunken behaviour.

In 1862 an American guide to alcoholic drinks gave a recipe for a spicy punch called 'Tom-and-Jerry'. In Britain, a low beer-house was called a 'Tom-and-Jerry' (1865) or a 'Tom-and-Jerry shop' (1873) – though there is some evidence that the term 'Jerry-shop' was already used in this sense before Egan's book appeared. The names became inseparably linked, so when a tomcat was made the protagonist of a cartoon series, it was inevitable that his mouse antagonist would be called Jerry.

Dermod Quirke, Halifax, West Yorks

Since the original book was *Three Men On The Bummel*, was this a mistake on the part of the enquirer or has literature fallen victim to the modern craze of down-sizing?

Are we to eagerly await the publication of A Gentlemen of Verona, Wuthering Height, A Tale Of One City and The Only Child Karamazov?

D. W. Cameron, Huddersfield

Was Asclepius, the ancient Greek physician said to appear in his patients' dreams and administer healing (often by performing 'surgery') man, myth, or both? And what is the explanation for the numerous 'offerings' (in the form of inscriptions on tablets or terracotta models of the healed body part or organ) supposedly left by grateful patients?

Asclepius was a myth, said to be the progeny of Apollo, a

god, and of Coronis, a mortal woman. Apollo's sister Artemis killed the pregnant Coronis but Asclepius was saved by post-mortem Caesarean section. Asclepius became a great healer. After he had been struck dead by Zeus he was resurrected as a god. His tale inspired Greek healers for centuries.

The healing temples originated about the sixth century BC. Many healing techniques were used including magic, drugs and surgery. Grateful patients then made offerings to the temple of terracotta. These were models of the part that had been healed, and common examples include limbs, breasts, ears and genitals.

The magic was effective for the same reason that almost any therapeutic procedure, orthodox or unorthodox, tends to help, especially if the patient has faith in the treatment. There is a placebo effect, a well-recognized psychosomatic phenomenon that should not be decried. In addition, time cures many diseases. This explains many cures claimed by healers of all kinds down the ages.

(Dr) Michael L. Cox, Higham-on-the-Hill, Warks

Asclepius may have been a myth, but the Egyptian Imhotep, who was identified with Asclepius, was definitely historical. Imhotep is recorded as holding the high offices of chief executive and master sculptor during the reign of King Zoser of the 3rd Dynasty (*c.* 2650 BC). It is likely that he was the architect of the king's tomb, the

Step Pyramid at Saggara — the first large building in the world to be built entirely of stone. After his death he was deified, and during the Graeco-Roman period (*c.* 332 BC to AD 395) he was worshipped as a god in cult centres and temples throughout Egypt. Imhotep's posthumous reputation as a healer at a time of Greek rule over Egypt led to the identification with the Greek Asclepius.

(Dr) Piotr Bienkowski, curator of Egyptian and
Near Eastern Antiquities, Liverpool Museum

I know that many nursery rhymes, such as 'Mary, Mary quite contrary', 'Little Jack Horner' and 'The Grand Old Duke of York' had origins based on historical fact. Is there any such explanation for 'Sing a song of sixpence'?

On a recent visit to Stockport's excellent hat museum (I really recommend a visit), I was informed that a 'weasel' in the line 'pop goes the weasel' is a tool used in hatting, and that 'popping' it referred to exchanging it for money at the pawnbrokers during times when there was a slow-down in work in the hatting industry. I assume that 'tuppeny rice' and 'treacle' were cheap food items that could be bought with the money.

Greg, Stockport, Cheshire

In Tudor times it was quite common to entertain the royal court by sticking something interesting in a pie crust. In fact if you go to Longleat house you'll see a statue of a dwarf who rose to prominence after jumping out of the king's pie.

Mark Blaker, Bristol

I've always wondered about this too. Perhaps it was a bit Cromwellian – dissolution of parliament etc., but that doesn't help with the maid's nose (rights being taken from 'the common people'?). As I'm sure you know, the bit about Jenny Wren's reinstatement of said nose is a modern, lily-livered addition. Does anyone know of the rhyme's earliest appearance?

Paula McClure, Dundee

The rhyme appears in volume two of *Tom Thumb's Pretty Song Book*, published around 1744. My favourite theory is that the twenty-four blackbirds baked in a pie represent the hours in a day. Opening the pie, and the birds singing, represents dawn and the dawn chorus. The King is the sun, the money is sunshine. The Queen represents the moon. Eating bread and honey is the waxing and waning of the moon. The maid in the garden hanging out the clothes may be a reference to clouds. It's a rhyme about the day.

Chris Lewis, Manchester

Who was the Green Man after whom so many pubs are named?

The Green Man appeared at May festivities hidden in a garland or bower of foliage or flowers in May Day celebrations based on ancient fertility rites. Also called Jack in the Green who appears in churches and cathedrals, on jetties of Tudor and other medieval buildings, he is a figure of medieval folklore, a symbol of the coming of spring, rebirth of vegetation and tree worship. He is usually given a sensual face with foliage growing from the mouth and curling around the head, carved in stone or made from oak.

Moira Brown, Dringhouses, York

When and how did the biblical cherubim, a class of angel who guard the gates to the Garden of Eden with flaming swords (Genesis 3:24) and who are described as terrifying creatures with multiple faces (Ezekial 10:8) become synonymous with the popular image of the cherub as a chubby child with feathered wings?

When cherubs are first mentioned in Genesis no indication is given of their shape or form, but according to Philo of Alexandria, the flaming swords mentioned signify the motion of the planets. Then in Ezekiel, they are actually described as 'chaiyoth' meaning 'living creatures', rather than terrible creatures.

As the second most powerful of the nine orders of angels, the cherubim, god's charioteers, are also accepted to have four wings and four faces: a lion, a man, a calf and an eagle, which represent the four elements, gospels, covenants or quarters of the globe, depending on who you believe.

It is worth remembering that much of the Old Testament is made up of apocrypha or stories passed down by word of mouth, which could have led to the confusion over their appearance. Egyptians placed a winged human figure over their sacred arcs, and the Persian bas-relief at Moung-Aub is a human figure dressed in an embroidered robe, 'with such quadruple wings as the vision of Ezekiel ascribes to the cherubim, with the addition of ample horns, the well-known symbols of regal power'.

As to the cherub's current image as a chubby child, the transformation is a mystery. These are figures from Greek and Roman mythology where the chubby infants with tiny wings are mischievous Cupids who use the power of love to bring both happiness and sorrow to human lives. The artists of the Renaissance simply combined this endearing pagan image with the biblical title and the result is millions of naked little fat boys fluttering around churches across Europe on diminutive wings. One of the most striking examples of this unlikely combination is Raphael's masterpiece, *The Vision of Ezekiel*, in which the artist ignores the prophet's description of the majestic cherubim and presents them as two cute little boys, holding up the arms of God.

Rob Mansfield, London SE27

What is the origin of the expression 'The man on the Clapham omnibus'?

The man makes his debut in the decision of Lord Justice Greer in the 1932 case of *Hall v Brooklands Auto-Racing Club*. He appears as that ubiquitous, and mythical, 'reasonable man' in order to set 'reasonable' standards.

In the case itself he is a spectator at a motor-racing event where a number of the watching crowd are seriously injured when a car careers through the barrier. To the question of whether the race organizers owed a duty of care to the victims he is made to reply with a firm negative, since 'he would know quite well' that no barrier would provide protection from this 'possible but highly improbable' occurrence. Thus the reasonable man denies any right of compensation.

Steve Silvester, Garstang, Lancs

While I do not doubt that Lord Justice Greer referred to the man on the Clapham Omnibus in his case of 1932, the fact is that he would have been referring to precedent. The first record of the man in question goes back to Lord Bowen in a case dated 1903.

Eric Ogden, Cheadle Hulme, Cheshire

The expression is generally attributed to John Burns (1858–1943), the Liberal MP and cabinet minister, a working-class Londoner by birth, and the man credited with the description of the Thames as 'liquid history'.

Francis Jones, London W5

In the *Journal of the Society of Arts* (May 1857), the following passage appears:

> So thoroughly has the tedious traffic of the streets become ground into the true Londoner's nature, that . . . your dog-collared occupant of the knife-board of a Clapham omnibus will stick on London Bridge for half-an-hour with scarcely a murmur.

How times don't change!

James W. Thirsk, Hadlow, Kent

Is Batman based on a true character?

The Batman, who first appeared in National Periodical's *Detective Comics* (May 1939), was created by Bob Kane (although some comic book historians now believe that the character was co-created with Bill Finger). The Comic Book Price Guide for Great Britain states that The Bat, a pulp fiction character of the early 1930s, was a direct antecedent of the Caped Crusader. While this is true, it should be noted that The Bat was loosely based on The Shadow, another popular pulp hero of the thirties and arguably the precursor for all modern superheroes.

Batman was not based on a real-life character, although there is a rumour that during the late 1910s there was a vigilante who patrolled the streets of the lower west side of New York, who was supposedly the son of rich parents inadvertently killed in a gangland slaying. But this is an apocryphal story and may have been told just as another reason behind Kane's inspiration.

Phil Hall, Comics International, Northants

Phil Hall's account of the Batman's origins omits two factors. Creator Bob Kane states in his autobiography that his two main influences for the Batman were Leonardo da Vinci's sketches of a man using a winged flying machine and Douglas Fairbanks' performance in *The Mark Of Zorro*. Moreover, the pulp character The Bat mentioned by Hall was adapted into a film, *The Bat Whispers*, and Kane lists Chester Morris's performance as the title character as another major inspiration. In this sense, Batman could be said to have been based on Fairbanks and Morris.

Will Brooker, Cardiff

Of Colin Dexter's Inspector Morse novels, why was *The Secret of Annexe A* the only one never to be televised?

In this novel Morse attends a New Year party in a small hotel. It is fancy dress and a person is murdered. There are only about ten people at the party and everybody is a suspect, including a man 'blacked-up' in the fancy dress of a Rastafarian. The killer turns out to be the Rastafarian, who is in fact a black man 'blacked-up' to try and convince everybody that he is white. Therefore, he would not be a suspect, because everyone at the party is white. I think you may find the answer to your query in there somewhere.

Clarry McDonald, London SW16

Why does Mickey Mouse wear gloves? Are there any films in which he isn't wearing them?

In *Plane Crazy*, made as a silent film in 1928 and released later with sound, Mickey is barefooted and barehanded.

Gallopin' Gaucho (again silent, 1928) sees Mickey in shoes for the first time and he kept them on for *Steamboat Willie*. The gloves came, I think, with either *The Barn Dance* (1928) or *The Opry House* (1929). As for the gloves, here's an explanation from Walt himself: 'We didn't want him to have mouse hands, because he was supposed to be more human. So we gave him gloves. Five fingers looked like too much on such a little figure, so we took one away. That was just one less finger to animate.' A very down-to-earth approach

Rolf Harris, Rolf's Cartoon Club, HTV West, Bristol

Hobbit, elf, troll, dwarf: what is the difference? And what is a good definition of a hobbit?

The first point is that the latter three are creatures with a long history in Germanic mythology, whereas hobbits are an invention of J. R. R. Tolkien. How does one tell the difference between the latter three? Elves tend to live in woodland, are as tall and thin as supermodels and immortal. They compulsively attract humans, generally to their doom. (Tolkien is a revisionist here: his elves are almost angelic compared to the traditional position, summed up in the Terry Pratchett lines 'Do Elves like mortals?' 'Yes, just like cats like a saucer of milk.')

Trolls live in mountain passes and below bridges. They

eat people and goats, are large, lumpish and stupid, and can be petrified by daylight. Dwarves live under mountains and are not immortal, merely quite long-lived. They make things from metal and are short and bearded. They are standoffish with a tendency to avarice. (Tolkien upheld the tradition here; Wagner on the other hand used his dwarves as a vehicle for his anti-Semitism.)

Hobbits, Tolkien's invention, were shorter than dwarves, slightly longer-lived than humans, fond of frequent good meals and possessed of proportionately large, thick-soled feet. They lived a pastoral and agrarian existence and in many ways were the heart of his 'Mythology for England'.

Stephen Allcroft, Dumbarton

They are easy to tell apart. Hobbits are small, narrow-minded and unimaginative. They read the *Daily Mail.* Elves are sanctimonious conservatives who don't much care about anyone else. They read the *Daily Telegraph.* Dwarves are grasping, humourless xenophobes. They read the *Financial Times.* A troll caught reading the *Sun* is generally regarded as a bit of an intellectual.

Steve Barton, Middlesbrough

PEOPLE AT PLAY

What is the most blatantly wrong decision ever made by a referee in a major football match?

After the February 1993 game between Oxford United and Sunderland, referee Stephen Lodge felt so guilty for wrongly dismissing a player that he reported himself to the F.A.

As far as one Italian punter is concerned, it has to be the referee who abandoned an Italian second division game in season 1996–7 in the eighty-ninth minute, denying the punter a 12-billion-lire win.

For dire consequences, it's a tie between the referee who allowed a disputed goal for Kaiser Chiefs against Orlando Pirates at Orkney (80 miles from Johannesburg) in 1991 that led to a riot in which forty people were killed and fifty injured, and the official who disallowed a goal in a Turkish championship match in 1967 resulting in an even larger riot with some six hundred injured and forty-one deaths.

Who'd be a referee?

Richard Webber (ex-class-3 referee), Bristol

At the end of the 1993–4 season, Bayern Munich's international Thomas Helmer scored an infamous goal against F.C. Nuremberg. He tried to tap in a low cross from inside the six-yard box, missed the ball and ended up in the net himself while the ball went out of touch. The players were about to get on with the match, but the referee (with a little help from the linesman) decided to give a goal, although the ball could not possibly have crossed the goal line and then gone out of touch.

Helmer did not tell the referee he had been wrong ('I am a professional footballer,' he said), but the whole match had to be replayed. Bayern won the match and thereby the league title.

Jan Tobiassen, Edinburgh

Blowing the whistle at kick-off.

Alistair King, Barcelona, Spain

Why do we kiss?

Ben Whitaker in his book *The Global Fix* states that

kissing is merely a way for lovers to test each other's semiochemicals. These are chemical substances that communicate biological signals between animals and which are produced by the sebaceous glands. Falling in love may only be a 'high' caused by addiction to another person's semiochemicals. Fortunately these drugs are not restricted under the Misuse of Drugs Act 1971.

Gill Kwik, National Drugs Intelligence Unit,
New Scotland Yard, London SW1

What is the logic behind racehorse names – and why did this tradition develop?

For some horses the logic is clear, such as in the case of Red Rum who was by QuoRUM (sire) out of MaRED (dam). Often this logic is enlivened with a certain amount of humour, so Dancing Brave and Shorthouse produce Lowawatha. Horses are also often named after the owner, a sponsor, or some other significant person or place.

Horse naming is controlled by Weatherbys (under contract from the British Horseracing Board) in the Register of Horse Names and there are strict rules about what counts as an acceptable name. Names cannot be more than eighteen characters, so Supercalifragilistic is a non-starter, but Supacalifragilistk was allowed. You cannot give a horse the same name of another living racehorse – up to the age of twenty – on the register (and within five years of its death; longer for brood mares and stallions).

No new horse name may be the same as, or close to, certain names on the International and Domestic Lists of Protected Names (the latter includes all the names of the winners of the ten major competitions in Britain), so however good an omen it might seem, you can't call your horse Aarkell because that is too near Arkle, nor Red Room (though there are three non-British horses registered with the name Red Run).

The Jockey Club also has rules banning names that are obscene, either in fact or implication. One might encounter difficulty in registering a horse called Fur Cough, for example. Names cannot be confusing, either. So Firstpassthepost could not be registered.

You may not name racehorses after 'public personalities' without their written permission, or that of their estate. All names must begin with a letter of the alphabet, so 'Eckythump could not be registered. Names cannot be formed from initials and figures.

Horses have informal names, too. Henrietta Knight calls Best Mate, 'Mate'. But even some official names have been prosaic: Eric, The Pub and Sean to name three. In the 1920s a horse called Toilet ran at Leicester (not terribly well).

The Queen has a well-deserved reputation for wittily naming horses. Feel Free was by Generous out of As You

Desire Me, and Rash Gift was by Cadeaux Genereaux out of Nettle. Other names are more opaque: Isidore Kerman's Kybo was named for his mother's habit of signing off letters to him at boarding school with the acronym KYBO, 'Keep Your Bowels Open'.

If all this seems rather eccentric, then you may take comfort from the fact that some owners have shown their exasperation with the naming system by giving horses names such as Itsnotnamedyet and Callitwhatyouwant.

If you have come up with a brilliant name then Weatherbys can reserve it for you, ready for the day when you finally get around to buying a horse . . .

Tim Gardner, Oxford

Although Weatherbys does its best to control names put forward for approval, this has often been seen as a challenge by owners and trainers. One major surprise came in 1989 when it allowed Who Gives A Donald, obviously unaware of the cockney rhyming slang term Donald Duck. In 1993, it took its eye off the ball again when approving Mary Hinge. Two of the most eye-catching names of horses still in training are Nobratinetta, sired by Celtic Swing out of Bustinetta, and Geespot, by Pursuit Of Love out of My Discovery.

The American commentator in New York had a field day in January 1993 when he excitedly announced: 'He's devoured the field . . . he's eaten up the opposition . . . he's had them for lunch,' when calling home the winner, Hannibal Lecter.

David Baxter, Holmfirth, West Yorks

If two people were running together at the speed of light, would they be able to see each other?

No. When running at that speed you dare not take your eyes off the road ahead.

G. A. Marshall, Edinburgh

The slugs in my garden always head straight past the weeds to dine on the leaves of my cultivated vegetables. Why is this, and could they be encouraged to eat the unwanted vegetation?

We have attempted to train slugs to eat the weeds in our garden with varying degrees of failure. Apart from the obvious fact of they're being finicky eaters, slugs simply prefer the more tender shoots in any garden.

We attempted to run seminars that extolled the virtues of weeds, their nutritional value and so on, but the slugs rarely showed up for these seminars and when they did, they meandered all over the place paying little or no attention to us as we spoke.

Another problem is that unlike humans, the slugs actually prefer fresh wholesome salad to anything else. The few slugs who were attentive and whom we were able to influence began to devour our hostas with a ferocity that shocked us.

In our next series of seminars, we paid no attention to their meanderings and spoke with the conviction of newly ordained ministers. Unfortunately our sunflowers were the next to go. With little or no positive response from the slugs we have finally given up and have decided to celebrate our defeat by inviting them to our own version of October Fest.

Bob Miller, Maine, US

Why are there no lady garden gnomes?

Ladies don't stand around in the garden all day doing nothing.

Marjorie Challis, Sutton, Surrey

The Gnome Reserve and Wild Flower Garden in West Putford, Devon, recently supplied me with a very nice lady gnome. This was a wedding gift for our next-door neighbours, who own a rather peripatetic male gnome.

The lady is obviously keeping him happy as the gnome
hasn't reappeared in our house or garden since.

Di Shaw, Horsham, Sussex

**In more than fifty years of concert-going, I've
never heard an instrumental player cough. How do
they stop themselves coughing? Are they expert
cough suppressors?**

Yes, we do cough during concerts. Usually, however, our
breathing is regulated in either playing brass/woodwind
instruments or (in my case) keeping time, so coughs are
avoided wherever possible. If one does happen to cough,
then the sound produced by the rest of the band is usually sufficient to drown it out.

Pooka, third percussionist, Bestwood Black Diamonds
Brass Band, Nottingham

Haven't you heard of a 'cacophony of sound'?

Dave Lambert, Harlow, Essex

The answer is simple. It's impossible to hear the players
coughing at a classical concert because of the competing
din of nose-blowing, throat-clearing, seat-shuffling,
unsuppressed sneezing, sweet-paper-unwrapping and
programme-dropping coming from the audience.

Unlike the questioner, I have only forty years' experience of concert-going, but the problem is getting worse (or I'm becoming less tolerant of audiences' inability to sit quietly) and I do begin to wonder whether it's worth attending live concerts any more.

Iain Williamson, Lytham, Lancs

Why do opera singers get so fat?

This is a popular fallacy. It is true there is still a belief among singers that an essential part of developing a powerful voice is to feed it. But the sylphic physique of many top female opera singers discounts this. There is always the odd Madam Butterfly or Mimi who weighs about 15 stone, but to opera enthusiasts it's the voice that matters. Male singers usually get away with anything because meat can be made to look like muscle.

Donald Barry, Bexhill-on-Sea, East Sussex

I am not so sure that opera singers as a whole get fat. It is some time since I have seen many overweight singers on the opera stage and, in fact, there are many examples of slim singers. Maria Callas springs to mind. The questioner seems to be thinking in stereotypes. If this stereotype could in any way be said to rest on fact, there could be a number of possible factors. At one time, of course, we had castrati, who naturally put on weight. Though this abominable practice ceased many years ago, it may have set the fashion for weightiness. Fat certainly used to be seen as strength in musical worlds (making you a better player, especially for people like brass players) and Louis Armstrong is a case in point. Classical music is very old fashioned in many ways. It could simply be that different standards of physical beauty, combined with an attitude that sound and ability are more important than appearance, let us see the full range of human physical variety on the opera stage (unlike female TV presenters).

I would think that if musicians do tend to fat as a whole, if not in detail, it would be due to their rather sedentary lifestyles. A professional musician can expect to spend a working day relatively immobile while concentrating all their effort on their playing. I have always found it rather odd that in a profession that is so concerned with physical control and development to exceptional lengths, that it literally produces a kind of athlete, but lets other areas of general health go by the board.

Jane Bennett, Manchester

Regretfully I must rubbish the rationalizers. Opera singers tend to put on weight because the thoracic expansion brought about by their rigorous exercises in breath control results in increased oxygen intake potential with its con-

comitant increase in appetite and the ability to digest —
and deposit as fat — more food. Channel swimmers, who
also incline to the chubby, are similarly affected but addi-
tionally employ thermal stimulation.

Red Daniells, Teddington, Middx

**Why is it that when I yawn around other people,
they too start to yawn? Is it contagious or is just
that everyone is tired?**

Yawning is one of the body's self-protection mechanisms.
During the course of everyday breathing you do not use
the extremities of your lungs and so they begin to close
permanently. Yawning ensures that they open regularly
enough to avoid closing. When you see someone yawn
it sparks a 'self-check' in the brain that says, 'Ooh, I'd
better do that too.' Why you yawn repeatedly sometimes I
don't know, maybe in case others aren't paying attention.

Alex Bird, Bournemouth

I once read that the more empathetic you are as a human
being, the more likely you are to yawn in response to
someone else yawning. It's like saying 'ouch' when someone else hurts themselves. It shows you care.

Alasdair Allan, Helensburgh, Scotland

AAAAAAAAWWWWWWW! Sorry, what was the question?

Marie Marshall, Dundee

When a newspaper ceases publication, as *Today* did on 17 November 1995, how do crossword fans find the solutions to that day's puzzle?

I'm not sure, but I've been stuck on 15 across for a hell of a long time!

Brad Jones, York

I'll swap you 15 across for 8 down.

Gary Farrell, Liverpool

Who was the best cricketer not to play for a Test country?

My father, the late Vincent Mather Thompson, who died recently, was captain of the first XI at Darlington Grammar School in the late 1930s. On leaving school, he was offered a place in the county side at Durham, but turned it down in favour of a career in the civil service. After the Second World War he played amateur cricket, including in the Lancashire League, until he was well into his late fifties (at which point he took up tennis!).

He captained every team he played for. He was a classical batsman – right-handed, with his left elbow pointing down the track towards the bowler – and a brilliant stroke player. I once saw him pull a short ball to the midwicket boundary; the ball bounced over the rope, continued bouncing over a tarmac playground the same width as the pitch, smacked against a wall and bounced back again.

Paul Thompson, Perth

The first class record of Frank Tarrant (1898–9 to 1936–7) is impressive: 17,952 runs at 36.41 and 1,512 wickets at 17.49 in 329 matches. Among more recent unlucky Australians I'd nominate Ian Brayshaw (1960–1 to 1977–8): 4,325 runs at 31.80 and 178 wickets at 25.08 in 101 matches, including only the third '10-for' in Sheffield Shield history; and Sam Trimble (1959–60 to 1975–6): 10,282 runs at 41.79 in 144 matches.

Jeremy Gilling, Sydney, Australia

There must be one or two South Africans from the seventies and eighties (who didn't become English, that is) that fall into this category. I nominate Ken McEwan, who hit 74 centuries and was a major player in Keith Fletcher's all-conquering Essex side which, along with Middlesex, dominated the English scene in the eighties. I'd also try a future nominee – Holland's Daan van Bunge. He scored runs aplenty in the World Cup as a teenager and could quite easily become the best-ever batsman from continental Europe.

Darren Beach, London

I would nominate J. Barton King, certainly the best American ever to play cricket. As a tourist he topped the English bowling averages in 1908 and scored 39 centuries in his career as a batsman. There are plenty of Australians nowadays who are superb at first-class level, but unlikely ever to play at Test level for Australia.

Darren Barfoot, Lancaster

Why are string instruments played with the most difficult and skilful work, i.e. the fingering, being done by the left hand and the easier, i.e. bowing, with the right hand, when most people are right-handed?

Anybody playing 'air guitar' will naturally use their main hand to strike the instrument and thus hold the guitar in the conventional way. I am left-handed and when I first took up the guitar in the sixties I held it in the way that seemed natural to me. Lack of progress and an adolescent desire for conformity led me to start again after a few months by learning to play right-handed. This was a real struggle – just picking the thing up was like trying to open a recalcitrant deck chair. I persevered and now I couldn't play any other way.

However, when it comes to 'air violin', I always hold the 'bow' in my left hand.

Wilko Johnson, Westcliff-on-Sea, Essex

I was fascinated by Wilko Johnson's contribution to the left-/right-hand string player debate. In the sixties, I played tea-chest bass for the Hot Street Syncopators, performing regularly on Canvey Island seafront as the pubs chucked out. Incidentally, being right-handed, I, conventionally, held the broomstick with my left and plucked with my right. Wilko, also a member of the combo, played acoustic guitar, harmonica, kazoo, comb and paper and occasionally, violin.

I still derive great pleasure from Wilko's masterful guitar playing, but admit to some relief to hear that he now limits himself to 'air violin'! Nevertheless, the mental image of Wilko 'air-duckwalking' to Vivaldi's *Four Seasons* may prove difficult to dispel.

Tony Maguire, Leeds

What is the longest uninterrupted 'dead' role where an actor has to lie on stage being, well, dead?

Some years ago, while playing Julius Caesar at the Bristol Old Vic, at the moment of death, an assassin's sword, serrated from the battle scenes, swept across my palm. As I crashed on the Capitol Steps I felt blood pouring from the wound. I then had to lie immobile for some five hundred lines sensing a pool growing around my hand. It may not be the longest an actor has had to pretend to be dead but it sure as hell felt like it.

Antony Tuckey, Ipswich

I'm not sure what the longest period was, but the shortest must be during the live CBS television broadcast of an adaptation of Raymond Chandler's *The Long Goodbye* on 7 October 1954, with Dick Powell as Philip Marlowe. The broadcast was marred by an actor playing a murdered man who, thinking the scene was over, got up and walked off the set in full view of the audience.

Richard Whitehead, Bury St Edmunds, Suffolk

As people are continuing to grow taller each generation, isn't it time we raised the basket in the game of basketball? When the game was first invented I'm sure the height of the basket was a challenge but if you look at a professional game in the N. B. A. it clearly isn't now.

Yes, the basket should be raised. In the same vein, the 22 yards set for a cricket pitch in 1744 is now disproportionately short compared to the current average height of a (male) cricketer. (It may be that the pitch is now in proportion for lady cricketers.)

Will Dunlap, Hamden, Connecticut, US

By admittedly bizarre comparison, even slightly tall people get backache when they're chopping vegetables, because the height of kitchen work surfaces was set to suit an average housewife way back when. The height is now fixed for all time, since dishwashers, washing machines and the like are all created to conform to this standard. Kitchen work surfaces are probably now four or five inches too low – a problem that can never be resolved, and which will become progressively more problematic with each (growing) generation.

Alan Paterson, London

I often hear it said that, on average, men are much more promiscuous than women. Given that there are roughly equal numbers of each, how is this statistically possible?

Excluding troilism, it is perfectly possible that fewer women than men are promiscuous, but that those few have a higher average number of partners. For example, one can imagine a small village where five out of twenty men have committed adultery, all with the same woman. Thus 25 per cent of men are promiscuous, compared with 5 per cent of women.

John Rogers, Bristol

Men lie because they consider being thought promiscuous a good thing. Women lie because they don't.

Peter Howe, Ryton, Tyne and Wear

Will the 100-metre-sprint record keep going down indefinitely or is there a theoretical limit to how fast the human body can move?

According to Feller's theory of records, the waiting time for a new athletic record doubles after each record is set. However, this assumes that there are no fundamental changes in the underlying population of athletes, which may not be true if the population becomes larger (a sport becomes dramatically more popular) or some other factor enhances performance over time (introduction of per-formance-enhancing drugs).

Although you cannot know that a particular record will never be broken, what happens at the limit of human per-formance is that records tend to get broken by smaller and smaller margins. Record-setting then becomes subject to debate about measurement methods, and tiny differences in competition conditions (even clothing) become highly significant.

Mitch Harris, Instow, Devon

What is the origin of playing cards? Who are the people on the face cards?

Playing cards originated in China, probably before the twelfth century AD, but underwent many evolutionary changes before reaching Europe (from the Mameluke empire) around 1360. The earliest European suits were headed by a king and two male officials, as they still are in traditional German, Italian and Spanish packs. The senior official was sporadically replaced by a queen in fifteenth-century Germany, but became standard only in the French suit system and its English derivative.

Court cards were not originally intended to represent anyone in particular, but the names subsequently attached to them in France, and still printed on them in traditional French packs, are: David, Pallas, Hogier (spades); Alexandre, Argine, Lancelot (clubs); Charles, Judith, Lahire (hearts); César, Rachel, Hector (diamonds).

David Parlett, author, The Oxford Guide to Card Games

The standard pictures on the face cards of the modern English pack began to be used in Tudor England before 1600. The earliest known English pack is a poor copy of one made in Rouen before 1516, so the tradition that the king of hearts is Henry VIII and his Queen is Anne Boleyn, complete with six fingers on her hand, or the queen of spades is Queen Mary with her consort Philip II of Spain as king of spades, is doubtful. Some of the symbolism matches with a French origin (orb with a Cross of Lorraine – but then kings of England were still claiming to be kings of France long after Calais was lost by Queen Mary).

Many modern card decks do attempt to include portraits of Henry VIII, Queen Mary etc., as reflected in Tenniel's court of cards in Lewis Carroll's *Alice in Wonderland*, where the mad queen is obviously based on Mary. Julius Caesar and Alexander the Great may also appear as kings.

The joker was apparently added after 1800 in Europe to support the game of euchre, and may only be coincidentally like the fool of the original trumps, and is definitely not drawn from James I's court jester Archy Armstrong, or the even ruder Sawney the Scot, who had a bit part in Macbeth. He looks more like Punchinello.

Ian Menz-McNicol, Höchst, Germany

When I listen to vinyl on a new, high-quality record deck, the sound produced seems to be warmer and more three-dimensional, and offers greater definition and far superior 'naturalness' of sound than that produced by a compact disc. Am I imagining this? If not, what are the reasons?

Any sound, including music, has a frequency (e.g., 400 hertz or 400 vibrations per second). When a note is played it is also accompanied by several harmonics at twice, four times, eight times etc., the base frequency (so our base note at 400 hertz will have its first harmonic at 800 hertz, its second at 1,600 hertz, third at 3,200 hertz etc.). Each harmonic usually has a smaller amplitude than the last. The more harmonics, the richer the base note will sound.

Since vinyl records are analogue they contain all the harmonics that accompany the note: the music is recorded as it sounds in the air with all the richness of the subtle smaller harmonics.

On the other hand, the music on a CD is compressed and the note is truncated after the first or second harmonic to save space. Result: the music on a CD does not contain the higher harmonics that give the subtle, rich texture to the music on a vinyl record. The difference is virtually imperceptible to most listeners and allows a lot more music to be stored on a small CD. But you obviously seem to have picked it up and no, you are not imagining it. Happy listening!

Hugh Burnham-Slipper, Bath

Most people are not such discerning listeners that CD sound bothers them. The problem is much worse with Minidisc and MP3. These leave out so much detail that only the most cloth-eared listener could regard them as high quality. The record companies seem to be worried by MP3, but nobody seems to be pointing out an obvious fact – it sounds crap!

John Rigg, Whitstable, Kent

Man U v Man C, Birmingham v Villa, Rangers v Celtic – even lowly Yeovil Town have sworn enemies in Weymouth FC. Can anyone name a football team that doesn't have a rivalry with another?

When I lived in Glasgow forty years ago you could be, and often were, stopped in the street and asked which team you supported. There was a 50 per cent chance of getting the answer right or suffering physical damage. The solution was to support Partick Thistle. So far as I know it had no foes and never won anything. But, of course, you were 'a ******* English *******' for supporting it.

I have supported Partick Thistle ever since.

Angus Doulton, Bletchingdon, Oxon

Partick Thistle have won the Scottish Cup (1921) and the Scottish League Cup (1971) among several other honours, but Angus Doulton is typical of the sort of 'support' they attract. This is an old Glasgow joke about the team.

'Are you going to see the Thistle this weekend, Tarquin?'

'I'd love to, Farquar, but there's a Fassbinder season on at the Glasgow Film Theatre.'

Of course, for some of us it's personal. Queen's Park were seven points clear at the top of the second division in 2000 when we ran across Thistle and their amazing synchronized diving displays. To cut a long season short, we dropped into the relegation zone for the first time on the very last day of the season. On goal difference.

Jim Steel, Glasgow

The recent survey by FootballFansCensus.com is incomplete: Gillingham F.C. does indeed have rivals in the form of Maidstone United. This is a long-standing rivalry exacerbated during Maidstone United's short stay in the football league when we regularly beat Gillingham. Though we are now in the Kent League, this rivalry still exists – in fact we are the Gillingham haters!

Trevor and Lyn Brockway, Maidstone, Kent

Trevor and Lyn Brockway write that there is a rivalry between Gillingham F.C. and Maidstone United. Isn't rivalry supposed to be a two-way thing? Maidstone supporters may well hate Gillingham, but Gillingham fans have more important things to worry about than a club as insignificant as Maidstone . . .

Russell Goodwin, Gillingham

Who first 'lost his bottle'?

Shakespeare wrote about lager louts in the early seventeenth century in *The Tempest*, Act IV Scene 1. After a drunken and fruitless chase across wild marshland led by the 'monster' Caliban, the bedraggled Trinculo bemoans the fact that he and Stephano have sunk so low as 'to lose our bottles in the pool'. Stephano agrees: 'There is not only disgrace and dishonour in that, monster, but an infinite loss.'

Colin Morley, Totteridge, London N20

The 'bottle' is, in full, the Cockney rhyming slang 'bottle and glass'. The 'loss' refers to the control of the anal sphincter in moments of great danger or stress. From this, we can deduce that Adam was the first to experience this unpleasant occurrence, when called to account in the Garden of Eden.

Joseph Cramp, Clayhall, Essex

It occurred to me recently that if Richard Littlejohn, Elton John and Little Richard were all standing in a row, they would form a kind of human palindrome. Can anyone really be bothered to think of another example?

I know both a Patrick Fitzgerald and a Gerald Fitzpatrick. I also know a Conor O'Connor who (almost) achieves a palindrome single-handedly.

Regen Holz, Dublin

Here's a footballing one: John Collins and Collins John both played for Fulham football club at the same time. To make it a bit longer you can add (if you like) Ronaldo of Brazil and Christiano Ronaldo of Portugal in the middle.

Haydon Bambury, Croydon

My name is Jon Dann. I used to go pubbing with two mates called Jon and Dan. Can you imagine the fun we had introducing ourselves to people? Dan, Jon, Jon Dann. Jon, Jon Dann, Dan. Jon Dann, Jon, Dan. Well, it was funny at the time . . .

Jon Dann, Lancaster

I have always thought that the word for a palin-drome should itself be a palindrome. My

suggestion is 'epitipe'. Now how do I go about getting this accepted as a new word in the English language?

Of course the word for a palindrome should itself be a palindrome. The suggestion of 'epitipe' has much to recommend it, but it may not elicit immediate recognition among all readers. May I suggest retaining loyalty with the current brand name, but altering it to 'palindromordnilap'.

I have always thought, moreover, that the word for an oxymoron should be an oxymoron. Any suggestions?

David Moon, Glasgow

You should write to: Sir Ron Norris
Ronam Manor
Evir Drive
Magnissingam
Nr Oxorn
E Fife

Alec Mitchell, Ashton-under-Lyne, Greater Manchester

I think either the process of creating a palindrome, or the state of being palindromic, should be called 'symme-temmys'.

As for David Moon's question about an oxymoronic definition of oxymoron: how about 'concordant contradiction'; 'antithetical synthesis'; 'converging divergence'; 'split union'; 'distant adjacents'; or 'agreeing opposition'?

Alex Dale, Lancaster

Does David Moon have an ultra-sly sense of humour? Is his follow-on query about the word 'oxymoron' a meta-textual illustration of the concept? 'Oxymoron' is an oxymoron. It means 'sharp-stupid'.

Rob Nash, London E2

I agree with the correspondence so far on palindromes, but I would like to add 'mononom' (one name either way) or 'monynom' as possible palindromic words for palindrome.

Robert Woolls, Horley, Surrey

'Epitipe', the new palindromic word devised to mean a palindrome, should be sent for official acceptance to the *OED*, citing the fact that the word was used with this meaning in the following poem by Adrian Mitchell, the shadow poet laureate:

> 'Lady Palindrome at work'
> Madam likes sweet peas,
> They're such a pretty pea.
> She tends them in her garden
> While composing an epitipe.

Of course if the questioner pronounces it to rhyme with kitty-wipe, he should forget it.

Adrian Mitchell, London NW5

As the palindrome and oxymoron discussions gather pace, let me add that 'pentasyllabic' is itself a pentasyllabic word.

Marcus Lynch, Clutton, near Bristol

Other matters perhaps worth pondering: Why does 'monosyllabic' contain more than one syllable? Why isn't 'phonetically' spelt phonetically? Is there another word for a synonym?

Katherine Clark, Southwell, Notts

In reply to Katherine Clark, phonetically is spelt phonetically, and so her question would appear to be an oxymoron. In which case, we are heading back where we started. Is this whole discussion, therefore, a metatextual illustration of the condition of palindromity?

David Moon, Glasgow

I haven't found a synonym for synonym, but its antonym is antonym.

Miranda Lewis, Sutton, Surrey

Has anyone else noticed that the word 'epitipe' is itself an epitipe?

David Deacon, London E4

I have always thought that the spelling of 'glottal' as in glottal stop, should be 'glo'al'.

Edward Brooks, Welwyn Garden City, Herts

To further the palindromic, oxymoronic and pentasyllabic debates, could I add that 'facetious' contains all the vowels, in their alphabetical order?

Brendan Cooper, London N8

Brendan Cooper's response was not complete. 'Facetiously' contains all six vowels, appearing only once and in alphabetical order. Ditto 'abstemiously'.

David Lane, Wakefield

'Facetious' has all the vowels in the right order. So has 'abstemious'. Perhaps at this juncture our logophiles may be a little more so in their scribaceousness.

Jeff Lewis, Exmouth

Could your 'abstemious' and 'facetious' correspondents all swallow a substance of an arsenious nature and put an end to it all?

Jimmy Jones, Liverpool

**Can anyone tell
Me if this
Is a poem or
not?**

Yes, it is a poem: a four-liner with a metrical pattern of sorts, based on the number of syllables it uses (5–3–5–1); in other words, it's an unrhymed syllabic quatrain, a form of poetry quite unusual in English (syllabic poetry is more commonly found in Japanese or the Romance languages).

However, in view of the ingenuous question the poem poses, it seems likely that the author thought he/she was writing something with no metrical pattern at all, i.e. so-called 'free verse'. This form, had it been realized, would have been very appropriate: because given the extremely banal nature of the poem's language and content, it is highly unlikely that any poetry reader would ever willingly pay to read it – unless, say, it was an ironically crude poem in an otherwise impressively written collection reflecting, among other things, on the nature of poetry.

Edward Martin, Bell, Eifel, Germany

The rhymes are good, the scansion sound, with words expressing thoughts profound. Only the layout seems to show it regards itself as prose not poetry.

no rhymes of
course never
heard of metre nothing to
say really but he
's got some tic in
his return-key
finger it'
s a poem.

Stephen Bond, Wädenswil, Switzerland.

Yes, it is a marvellous poem. It is jaunty and playful. Its hopscotch syncopation portrays a jurring dance punctuated by the poet's wide leaps. May we hear more?

Robert Bruker, Gallup, New Mexico

This question, and others like it, seems to demand an answer by reference to the necessary and sufficient conditions of something's being 'X' – in this case a poem. But some concepts can spring an intellectual trap on the unwary – the attempt at definition launching them upon an endless philosophical round of theory and counter-example. This is a fun game played by philosophers for some three thousand years or more now. But alternative approaches exist.

Confronted with such questions as 'what is art?', Wittgenstein suggested that we first ask not for the meaning of the concept, as supposedly elucidated by a list of necessary and sufficient conditions, but for the use that it receives in everyday discourse. He intended this tactic to dissolve the problem of definition by presenting a pragmatic insight into how (and thereby why) people use the words they do.

Wittgenstein's contention was that rather than being based upon an underlying set of semantic conditions the use of concepts in language has a strictly pragmatic rationale. In other words, there exists no 'theory of art' to be uncovered by quibbling philosophers, because people's use of the term is not at any level – even the level of sophisticated art critics – grounded in theory.

In this respect, it has to be conceded that Wittgenstein's view appears to account neatly for the continued failure of philosophers over a period of some three thousand years to reach a consensus on the major questions of their subject.

With regard to the question posed, it is necessary to consider the probable judgments of readers encountering it in different contexts. A poetry reader encountering Doyle Cross's effort in the pages of a modern-day collection or anthology would, I suspect, be inclined to allow that it was a poem – if only on the grounds that in light of the stylistic and typographical innovations occurring in the past century or so of poetry's development, there can remain no literary conventions governing 'what counts as poetry' which would be strong enough to disbar it from that status.

That said, the verdict of listeners at a poetry reading who had the same form of words read to them would, I suggest, be to the contrary. As would that of debaters of the following: 'This house believes/That this motion is/Not poetry/In motion/So much as a/Motion in poetry.'

If so, this would in turn suggest that in extreme instances the parameters governing what counts as poetry vary across written and spoken forms of expression. If the history of poetry is charted as the transition from a predominantly oral form to a predominantly written one, the innovations of the past century can be viewed as the evolutionary sloughing off of the final residual conventions governing the process.

Matthew Wilson, Ongar, Essex

If you call
Yourself
A poet,
Then yes.

Carolina Denning, Leeds

Babies' toys are all bright primary colours, but babies seem to prefer to play with black objects

like remote controls and mobile phones. Has a black toy been successfully marketed to infants?

This is nothing to do with the colour of the object but is more to do with the babies copying the parents' actions.

Graham Park, Abergavenny, Monmouthshire

Black-and-white toys for babies are readily available and are rather popular among parents who are in the know. Examples include picture books, soft building blocks, stuffed toys and mobiles.

In the earliest months of life, the visual cortex is developing representations of the most basic visual phenomena such as edges and lines. Simple visual stimuli, such as straightforward geometrical or circular patterns and strong contrasts (e.g. black against white), serve these needs best. Even patterns of colour are too complicated to interest the infant very much. For the first few months of her life, our daughter had a black-and-white mobile hanging over her cot, which never failed to produce smiles and excited leg and arm movements.

(Dr) Shan Parfitt, Klosterneuburg, Austria

What is the earliest evidence of human beings having a sense of humour?

Professor Raymond Dart, the South African paleontologist who discovered Australopithicus, gives an account of the discovery of a pebble found in a cave in 1925 that appears to have been carried there from a river bed at least 20 miles from the cave. When looked at one way up it displays an inane lopsided grin, while turned upside down it looks like the serious face of a man with a hat.

Neville Grenyer, Bristol

The human sense of humour goes back at least 15,000 years when, inevitably perhaps, it was lavatorial. A palaeolithic spear-thrower, carved from reindeer horn and found at a Magdalenian site in France, depicts an ibex in the act of defecation. Furthermore, the surprised animal has turned its head to observe that a bird has alighted on the emerging excrement.

Bill White, Chesham, Bucks

The Flintstones.

Paul Palmer, Ellesmere Port, Cheshire

Inventing the wheel before inventing the road.

Peter Mcpartland, Liverpool

Bob Monkhouse's joke-book.

Adam Hogg, Lesmahagow, Lanarks

In the Archaeological Museum of Iraklion stands a beautiful vase dated around 1600 BC that depicts workers returning from the harvest. Full of song and full of wine, the figures are shown marching home. Looking carefully, one can see a figure facing backwards and laughing heartily. On the ground behind him one of the workers, drunk on raki, had stumbled and fallen amidst this orderly procession.

Paul McAfee, York

Why don't women go fishing?

Because they have more sense.

Judith Ward, Newcastle-under-Lyme, Staffs

There are a few women who go fishing, but it is true that men are in the majority where this activity is concerned. The reason for this is that fishing involves killing or hurting something for fun. This is of course perverse and there are fewer female perverts than male ones.

Hazel Tarragon, Shrewsbury, Shrops

Because women go shopping and get their fish from the fish shop. This time-efficient strategy leaves us free to do our knitting.

Josie O'Farrell, Liverpool

As an angler of many years' standing I can state that the reason is, quite simply, that there are no lavatories on the riverbank. This was highlighted for me just recently when my stepdaughter asked to come fishing with me.

Adrian Wood, Brightlingsea, Essex

There's a big answer to this one. Fishing belongs to a wide category of activities (including hobbies such as stamp-collecting and bird-watching and 'passions' such as football) that Sigmund Freud called 'displacement' activities, implying that people engage in them to compensate for not being able to do what they really want. In other words, our true nature is being repressed and channelled into fundamentally irrelevant sideshows (among which, incidentally, he included higher intellectual activities such as the arts and sciences). Freud used this, among other arguments, to demonstrate that civilized society is in contradiction with our instinctual selves and spawns not only these activities but also a vague, deep-rooted unhappiness.

Typically androcentric, Freud never observed that women do not, generally speaking, share these activities. If he had, he might have concluded that women do not require such absorbing displacement activities because their true natures are not repressed to the same extent as men's. They are more in tune with their drives than men.

Of course, what men would rather be doing is probably unspeakable, which is why their instinctual natures were repressed by society in the first place. Social conditioning is such that men themselves are usually unaware of what they really want. So they go fishing, and women don't.

Nick Growse, Vitrac, France

Who tested the first parachute and did he live to tell the tale?

Disregarding Chinese acrobats who, in order to entertain the emperor in the sixteenth century, were supposed to have jumped from various heights with umbrellas attached to themselves, and Fausto Veranzio of Venice who is supposed to have tested a crude form of parachute in 1616, it is generally accepted that Sebastian le Normand of Montpellier in France was the first person to test a parachute. This he did on Boxing Day in 1783, jumping from the tower of Montpellier Observatory, attached to a rigid parachute made of canvas and wickerwork. He landed safely.

The originator of the folded parachute, capable of being stored in a container and opening on descent, was Major Thomas Baldwin of the US who, in 1850, began successful demonstrations of his equipment by dropping from a balloon. However, the parachutes suffered from the limitation that they were attached to the balloon and were opened only by means of the parachutist dropping away, pulling the parachute from its container and, when fully extended, breaking the cord attaching the parachute to the balloon. The reputed inventor of the self-contained, manually opened parachute capable of being worn about a person's body was Leo Stevens of the US who, in 1908, is said to have demonstrated such a parachute, though it was not until the First World War that such parachutes became generally available.

Steve Day, Salisbury, Wilts

If I were to throw three darts randomly, all landing within the scoring zone, what score should I get?

'Random throwing' is an impossible task — the writer would have to aim, initially at the correct wall, probably for the bull, and depending upon his skill, there would be a distribution pattern biased towards the centre of the board. However, it is possible to imagine a machine firing darts at a wall, of which the dartboard is part, and using randomly chosen vertical and horizontal coordinates, from which only 'hits' are used. The following answer will then apply.

A dartboard has six annular zones (double, outer, triple, inner, 25 and 50) and, according to my measurements (and a little bit of rounding) the areas as a percentage of the whole are: 10.25, 51, 7, 30.5, 1, and 0.25. The segmentation of the board can be ignored by using the average value of the numbers from 1 to 20, which is 10.5. Combining these numbers (e.g. a 7 per cent chance of scoring 21 [a double 10.5]) gives a score of just over 13.63 per dart, or nearly 41 for three. In real life (e.g. at a fairground stall where challenges to exceed a certain number (40?) to win a teddy bear are commonplace) this challenge can be won with skill, or, more likely lost by virtue of misses or darts falling out of the worn-out board.

Ian Tanner, Market Deeping, Peterborough

Assuming three darts are thrown completely randomly within the scoring area of a standard darts board, the average score per dart is 14.6, giving a likely average total of 43.8 for the three. If your aim is up to consistently landing within a smaller area, then the average can be increased by aiming at the right section of the board. For instance, if you can narrow your aim to a quartile of the board, aiming at the segment from 17 through 16 would give an increased average of 16.63 per dart.

Quite why the average should increase still further after a pint or two is, however, open to question.

Steve Antill, Wednesbury, West Mids

I have played darts for many years with players of all levels, from beginner to professional. I have always concluded that while a good player will average 60 plus, a moderate player 45–60 and a relative newcomer around 40–45, a complete beginner who is happy just to hit the board will usually average 35.

Jim Pickard, Clacton-On-Sea, Essex

Who was the first April Fool?

The tradition of the trickster in northern Europe goes right back to our pre-Christian religion. In the Norse mythology, the prankster-god Loki can be disruptive towards the other gods but able to carry out tasks no other can. He represents the need to question and challenge authority so that patterns of thought and behaviour do not become stale or accepted uncritically. Loki is traditionally thought of as patron god of April.

Andy Lawton, Chesterfield, Derbys

My wife is a runner and I am a cyclist. My wife has run a marathon. How far must I cycle to equal this feat?

I am a cyclist and a runner who has done a marathon.

There is no amount of cycling you can do that will equal the pain of dragging aching legs over the last 10 miles of a marathon. Congratulations to your wife.

Paul Francis, Muscat, Oman

Colleagues at my running club who combine running and cycling have always maintained there is a four-to-one ratio between cycling and running distances. According to them, you would have to cycle slightly under 105 miles to complete the equivalent of a marathon on your bike.

Hugh Mooney, Glasgow

Why are tennis players given two chances at one of the most fundamental elements of the sport – serving? Footballers don't get second chances at free kicks, corners, etc., and surely only one chance would make tennis more entertaining.

Lawn tennis is based on the courtly game of real tennis. There, a serve may be of such complexity that one is forgiven for making a hash of it and allowed another go. However, if a player's serve falls out of play simply because it was hit too hard, there is no second serve. The rule works well and the game allows a number of other ways to score outright winners during the course of play.

Stephen Pardy, London SE11

I expect the second serve is a hangover from the amateur era, where it was probably appropriate. To even up the difficulty factor, why not also eliminate the net cord replay? Such changes would favour technical skill over sheer power and undoubtedly be good for the game.

John Bentley, Huntingdon

What a good idea! Yes, let's introduce second chances at free kicks and corners in soccer. There will need to be some discussion on the details of when the second attempt is allowed, but it would lead to more goalmouth excitement from the extra corners, and give another chance of punishing a team who commit fouls just outside their own penalty area.

A better suggestion for tennis is that it moves closer to the squash rule, whereby the receiver can opt to accept a foul serve. In tennis, if the first serve is too long, or too wide, the receiver is allowed a free hit at it: if the receiver's return is not good, the second serve proceeds as now; but if the return is good, and not returned, the point is won by the receiver. Finally, if the return is good, and the server's second shot is also good, the receiver now either 'accepts', i.e. makes an attempt to play the ball – the game is in progress, or 'rejects', i.e. makes no attempt to play the ball, and the current second serve rule pertains.

This is not as complicated as it may look.

John Haigh, Brighton

Stephen Purdy says that in real tennis if a serve is hit too hard and falls out of play there is no second serve. But the 1999 revision of the Laws of Real Tennis states at 11.2(b) 'a player loses a point if as server he serves two consecutive faults for that point'.

In France, I believe, they still play the old rule where a serve dropping beyond the half-court line is not treated as a fault but as a pass (like a let in lawn tennis) but in the rest of the world two service attempts are allowed.

Nick Clayton, Alderley Edge, Cheshire

Personally, I could do with three.

Ron Southey, Deal, Kent

PEOPLE AT WORK

People sometimes use the phrase 'it's not rocket science' when they want to refer to something that should be straightforward, but what do people who work for Nasa say in similar situations, when everything they do is in fact rocket science?

Rocket scientists never use the common expression, because they know better than anyone that rocket science is the simplest science there is. As Isaac Newton pointed out, 'for every action there is an equal and opposite reaction'. In other words, throw something one way and you will be pushed the other way (think of the kick from a rifle when it is fired). That's all there is to rocket science — throw stuff out one way, and the rocket moves the other way.

Of course, rocket technology is a lot more complicated.

A better term would be: 'It's not quantum physics.' Now, quantum physics really is hard!

(Dr) John Gribbin, University of Sussex

In the same spirit as John Gribbin, I have for some time now used the phrase 'We're not talking wave/particle duality here'. It sometimes causes confusion but frequently moves the conversation on to something more interesting.

John Haggerty, Wirral, Cheshire

I saw a photo in a magazine a while ago of Buzz Aldrin wearing a T-shirt with the words 'No, I really am a rocket scientist' on it.

Karen McCarthy, Birmingham

We know about MI5 and MI6 but were there ever an MI1 to MI4? If so, what did they do? And do they still exist?

I could tell you, but then I'd have to kill you.

Neil Badmington, Cardiff

MI1 – director of Military Intelligence; also cryptography
MI2 – responsible for Russia and Scandinavia
MI3 – responsible for Germany and Eastern Europe
MI4 – aerial reconnaissance during the Second World War

MI5 – domestic intelligence and security
MI6 – foreign intelligence and security
MI8 – interception and interpretation of communications
MI9 – clandestine operations, escape and evasion
MI10 – weapons and technical analysis
MI11 – field security police
MI14 – German specialists (I wonder if this still exists . . .)
MI17 – secretariat body for MI departments
MI19 – PoW debriefing unit

Yes, this is correct. I don't understand the numbering system either. Bear in mind that these are only the ones that MI has let on about. Perhaps the six missing ones are in charge of creating departments that don't exist, hiding ones that do exist, finding departments that people have left in taxis . . . who knows? Cue Twilight Zone music . . .

Olwen Lachowicz, London W12

Why do even 'smart' people take a pride in the fact that they were 'never any good at maths', while they would never confess to having problems reading? Why is innumeracy acceptable?

The questioner makes one fundamental error in confusing innumeracy with being bad at mathematics. Numeracy is an important, yet mundane, skill, while mathematics is a wonderful, creative, beautiful, exciting, exotic, surprising and amazing journey of discovery; the two have little in common.

The paradox of mathematics is that, while its formal methods are the acme of logic, the process of its development and expansion is one of pure creativity, having as much to do with imagination as logic. It is one of the great intellectual tragedies that so few people are able to break through the fog of prejudice and scale the mountains of intellectual rigour required to appreciate this most wonderful of intellectual pursuits. Those who take pride in their lack of understanding of mathematics are cutting themselves off from one of the oldest and yet still most vigorous aspects of human culture.

Chris Hewitt, Aberteifi, West Wales

Mathematics is possibly one of the hardest subjects it is possible to study, of which ignorance is excusable, though not something to be proud of; but numeracy, a basic skill of life and a tiny fraction of mathematics, is something anyone should be ashamed not to know.

Donald Baillie, Penicuik, Midlothian

At boarding school, to combat boredom, I spent weekends solving problems in geometry with the aid of theorems. Though a maths freak, I was considered useful in times of pre-exam stress.

Geometry was applied by ancient Egyptians to solve irrigation difficulties along the Nile valley long before the Greek Pythagoras opened up his academy. In spite of achieving fame during his lifetime, Pythagoras was himself a social outcast, who ended up being burnt to death by a tyrant, along with his academy.

This summer at the seaside I read *Fermat's Last Theorem*, which I found more exciting than any crime novel. My friends wondered about me. My daughter exclaimed: 'But Mummy, it's full of formulas!' The moral is: keep quiet if you can prove why a3 + b3 = c3 is incorrect. You'll be ostracized, if not burnt at the stake!

Sylvia Maclagan, Buenos Aires, Argentina

I'm trying to figure it out.

Bob Holderness-Roddam, Austins Ferry, Tasmania

Is mathematics invented or discovered? If the latter, who made the discovery?

Mathematics, in my opinion, is the expression of the physical and metaphysical truths that surround us (and always have). We have invented the language with which we describe the patterns we recognize but we have not caused them to be true. Only the creator (whatever name you use for this entity) has the power, cleverness and clearness of thought to create a physical law at will.

Martin Fournier, Mississauga, Canada

Just as the ability to formulate grammar seems to be embedded in genetic code, it is entirely possible that a mathematical order is embedded in the universe – something that we are discovering. We may not have perfected the tools (such as the decimal system or binary code) but no one can deny that certain parameters relate with others in a defined way. If mathematics is a tool then we also 'discovered' that tool. I would suspect our earliest agricultural ancestors discovered mathematics and I would suspect the moon's waxing and waning would be the source of that discovery.

M. Calvin, London

Mathematics is both invention and discovery. The language of mathematics (such as addition and fractions) is an invention. The things that the language describes (such as Pythagoras's theorem) are discoveries. Both strands make up mathematics.

Peter Brooke, Kinmuck, Aberdeenshire

Mathematics is a finite series of abstract, two-dimensional symbols invented by humans, arranged and rearranged according to a set of rules and procedures also invented by humans. When all the procedures have been carried out and the rules adhered to, an answer is produced. By this method humans delude themselves into believing that they are revealing the secrets of the universe. If you change the familiar symbols of mathematics to bones or tarot cards, you have magic and witchcraft. It is all the same.

Incidentally, John Maynard Keynes once said of Sir Isaac Newton and his *Principia Mathematica* that he was not so much the first of the great scientists as the last of the great magicians.

J. Owens, London

French onion men were a feature of my fifties childhood. They rode around on bicycles selling strings of onions. Where did they come from, and what's happened to them?

The onion sellers hailed from the Roscoff region of Brittany. Spending the growing season in France, they would travel to Britain during the autumn and winter because the British were said to pay more for their onions than the French. During their heyday the sellers would charter their own boats to carry the crop to Britain. On arrival, they lived in hovels surrounded by mountains of onions to be thread on raffia strings.

Each team of men (and women) would travel to the

same area of Britain each year. They were particularly numerous in all areas of Wales, where they were often called *Sioni Winwns* (Johnny Onions). Some still travel from Brittany but they are few in number.

Eryl Crump, Bodorgan, Gwynedd

Does anyone know what is the most successful film ever, in terms of return on investment, based on receipts against cost of production?

According to CNN it was a film called *Deep Throat* starring a Ms Linda Lovelace, which was made in six days for $25,000 (£13,000) and has allegedly grossed more than $600m (£320m). I haven't seen it myself, ahem . . .

Darren Barfoot, Lancaster

Do great minds think alike?

Yes, but only if yours is as great as mine.

Peter Mellor, City University, London EC1

Only when mine is one of them.

Rob Parrish, Teignmouth, Devon

Einstein, I understand, believed that no two great thinkers

thought in exactly the same way. (This may have something to do with his being dyslexic – dyslexics are famous for their idiosyncrasy.) Edison, however, held that great creative thinkers shared certain fundamentals in terms of how they functioned. So, apparently not!

Simon Hopper, Bromley, Kent

Surely the essence of a great mind is that it is original and unique.

Lucie Keeton, Meltham, Holmfirth

The very question I was going to ask. See you at the Mensa AGM, Norm.

David Donnell, London SW14

According to, among others, the Buddhists and the late Bill Hicks, we are all 'one consciousness experiencing itself subjectively'. In this case, perhaps the question should be: 'Does great mind think alike?'

Nick Barber, London SW6

Do great minds think alike?

Anthony Venditti, London E18

Well, fools seldom differ . . . I wonder how many of us said that?

Mark Johnson, Coventry

What does a 'best boy' do for his living and what is a 'chief grip'?

The best boy is a senior electrician on a film crew, coming second in the hierarchy to the 'gaffer', the chief electrician. The electricians are responsible for the technical side of the lighting and are known as the 'sparks' in this country or 'juicers' in the US.

In the US the chief carpenter on the set is sometimes known as the 'key grip' but here the term refers to the head of the team known as 'grips', which is responsible for the camera support equipment (tripods, etc.). This includes pushing the 'dolly' for a tracking shot, an important job as the grips are in direct contact with the shot and one little jolt is seen by everyone.

The terminology often reflects the traditions of sexist hierarchy that were very common in the industry. Things are changing, so it is possible to have mature women as best boys, or mature men as continuity girls. We still use portable lights known as 'blondes' and 'redheads'.

Nick Burton, Christ Church College, Canterbury

Is it morally right for a lawyer to defend a client despite knowing that the client is guilty?

Yes. Although the nature of the defence must be clarified.

If the client tells us that he/she is guilty, there are two ways of 'defending' the case. The first is upon a guilty plea, defending a client's interests by way of mitigation.

Second, a client may be defended by getting the prosecution to prove its allegation. It is morally right that the state should be required to prove its case against those whom it seeks to prosecute. To allow anything less than proof would be wholly unacceptable.

This process of 'putting to proof' is closely connected to the issue of the right to silence. Any legal right or freedom is a building block in the overall morality of a society, even when such a right or freedom may enable the individual to act with something short of full personal morality.

Tim Rose (defence solicitor), Bristol

No. The principles under which I have operated as a criminal defence lawyer for the last twenty-four years have been as follows:

If the client says that he is not guilty, then I accept at face value his instructions, and I will defend him to the best of my ability. If the evidence against him is so overwhelming that he will be convicted in any event, I will always point out clearly the risks that he faces, but the decision must always be that of the client. If he persists in his denial, then I will continue to defend him.

If a client tells me that he is guilty, but he is going

to put forward a defence, I will show him the door forth-with.

If a client admits to me his guilt and subsequently admits it to the court, I have no moral qualm at all about representing him (not 'defending him'), so that all that is good about him (if anything) can be said to the court.

Roger Corbett, Birmingham

If all human beings disappeared from the Earth tomorrow, how long would it take nature to remove all traces of human existence?

Oh, for goodness sake, why do you need to know that?

Juliet Abrahamson, Linton, Cambridge

The short answer is: almost certainly never. Cultivated land, gardens and parks would be the first human achieve-ments to return to nature, though even they would take fifty years or so to become invisible to the casual observer. Wooden structures would fall next, rotting in around a hundred years. Anything built of brick, stone or similar material would take much longer to decay, depending on its precise make-up; paving slabs, concrete runways, motorways and other large flat areas would break up in perhaps a century and a half.

It is the great human constructions in steel, glass and

reinforced concrete that have real staying power. Requiring essentially zero maintenance as far as structural integrity is concerned, a modern skyscraper might (earthquakes aside) last for several centuries, while a hydroelectric dam such as the Hoover – made from millions of tonnes of virtually solid concrete that took decades to actually set – would last much longer. Even after a thousand years, traces of most of these would remain, just as we can detect the shadows of Iron Age settlements under present-day fields.

Chris Rogers, Edgware, Middx

Most surface traces of human activity would probably be gone within about ten thousand years. Within a few decades, a forest covering would be well on the way to being re-established, with many buildings still standing between the trees, as places like Chernobyl, Beirut and Second World War bomb sites in many European cities have shown.

Fallen leaves and new undergrowth would recreate a soil base to hide roads and other barren surfaces, as tree roots, erosion and occasional floods slowly demolished most buildings. Traces of Roman villas could still be seen for about a thousand years after the Romans left, albeit after attentions by building-stone robbers.

Some concrete atom bomb shelters would last much longer, though, becoming increasingly hard to find in the forest, like the Mayan temple ruins. The Egyptian pyramids, in a more arid area, have lasted a few thousand years and will likely last quite a few more millennia before being sandblasted away or buried in dunes.

Earthworks such as railway cuttings and embankments would last longer, as have relics such as Offa's Dyke. Eventually, soil movements caused by tree roots, badgers, rabbits and moles would smooth these out, too.

Last to go would be deep, underground structures such as railway and MoD tunnels. These would leave 'fossil' traces, as would actual dead humans. The only way nature will remove such 'fossils' is by subduction of the crust that they lie in back into the earth; the ultimate in terrestrial recycling.

We cannot know when the last human-related 'fossil' will be so subducted, but there are rocks today on Earth dated at around 4 billion years old, almost the age of the earth itself (4.5 billion years). These rocks will likely be here for a billion or two years more, as they are in stable crustal areas like central Canada, far from any active subduction zones.

Perhaps it will take until the sun runs out of hydrogen and explodes in around 5 billion years' time to destroy the Earth and all traces of humanity. However, new research suggests the Earth may just survive this event, as by then the sun will be less massive and the earth will orbit further out than now. The Earth's core will cool and subduction will cease. In that case, the last traces of human activity will survive terrestrial life and 'nature' itself. They will linger on till the end of the universe.

(Dr) Hillary Shaw, Leeds

Slightly less time than if the contract were awarded to Liverpool city council.

Peter Bradshaw, Liverpool

When we encounter intelligent extraterrestrial beings, what should be the first Earth music we play to them?

It depends whether we want to embrace or repel them. (Insert your own Lloyd-Webber joke here.)

Mark Power, Dublin

After gaining office, how long does it take for politicians to go bonkers?

The *Washington Post* columnist David Broder said in 1973: 'Anybody that wants the presidency so much that he'll spend two years organizing and campaigning for it is not to be trusted with the office.' The answer would appear to be two years prior to the election.

Brian Robinson, Brentwood, Essex

Are there any recorded instances of surgeons performing operations on themselves?

Yes, although DIY operations aren't limited to surgeons. With the permission of a hospital in Colorado, Dr George Balderston removed his own appendix. In March 1978 he sat in the hospital's surgical theatre, anaesthetized himself, opened up his abdomen and snipped and closed the wound with clamps and stitches unaided within an hour.

For unqualified DIY operations, however: In 1993 Poppy Faldmo, 21, of Salt Lake City, took out her own tonsils because she didn't have medical insurance to cover the £700 hospital bill. She spent hours every day in front of a mirror, removing the inflamed tonsils a little at a time with nail scissors and a modelling knife, using a toothache gel as an anaesthetic. Doctors say she did a perfect job.

Stephen A. Graham, Carlisle, Cumbria

As a dental surgeon I have, on two occasions, extracted an offending tooth from my own mouth.

H. H. Reeves, London SW11

The bow and arrow was a traditional weapon in Mesopotamia, New Guinea, South America and Europe. How did it become so widespread across the world? Did it spread from a single centre or was it invented independently in various places?

It is not only the bow and arrow – larger artefacts such as pyramids around the world (for example those at Teotihuacán in Mexico, and at Giza in Egypt – and note that there are other pyramids in North America, Europe and Asia) have uncanny similarities that traditional narratives of history fail to explain.

There is some evidence to suggest that traditional accounts of history may be wildly inaccurate, and that ancient races (e.g. ancient Meso-Americans and ancient Egyptians) might have had the capability and the technologies for global trade and communication. Professor Svetlana Balabanova, curator of the Egyptian mummies in Munich, found traces of tobacco and cocaine in samples of hair taken from her mummies. Professor Rosalea David in Manchester conducted similar experiments on mummies there, with the same results.

Since tobacco and cocaine are plants indigenous to the Americas, we might conclude that global trading was, contrary to traditional thinking, practised in ancient times, and that the widespread adoption of specific and useful technologies such as the bow and arrow may therefore be less mysterious than traditional accounts would suggest.

Tom McMaster, Manchester

The universality of the bow and arrow has to be qualified in order to answer this question. As with other human technologies, two reasons can be given for the apparent ubiquity of this weapon: 1) An inherent technical logic leading from more primitive ballistics, e.g. the spear launcher (*atlatl*) or sling shot, to independent invention among different peoples around the globe; 2) Cultural diffusion, e.g. as migrants spread knowledge among previous non-users.

Unfortunately for these theses, the 750,000 Aboriginal people of Australia have never used the bow and arrow, even though they seem to have known of its existence.

Aborigines are known to have made use of the bow drill as a fire-maker. Also, in the far north of Australia, children were given bows and arrows as toys. The theory is that these were acquired by trade with the bow and arrow-wielding islanders who inhabited the Torres Strait between Australia and New Guinea.

However, the Aborigines' lack of any serious interest in the bow and arrow suggests it only became a must-have weapon elsewhere under two conditions: 1) When it fulfilled a unique ballistic use that other hunting technologies could not – the Aborigines were able to rely on spears, boomerangs and fire-traps; 2) In 'arms race'situations:

when competition and conflict with other peoples who already used the bow and arrow as a military weapon dictated reciprocal adoption by previous non-users – a threat that the Aborigines, largely isolated from other peoples for at least 40,000 years, did not have to face.

Bryn Jones, Bath, Somerset

Why do catwalk models look so miserable?

I don't know when it became de rigueur but the fashion model scowl was identified at least half a century ago. In Jean-Paul Melville and Jean Cocteau's 1949 film version of Cocteau's novel *Les Enfants Terribles*, the terrible twin Elizabeth (Nicole Stéphane) is coached by her friend Agatha in how to comport herself as a fashion-house mannequin:

> You approach from a distance, face the customer, hands on hips, thumbs forward, stare into her eyes with a nasty look. You stop, turn your back slowly, face her again, you inspect her from head to toe as if you didn't see her. Then, with a scornful look, you walk away.

Thus prompted, the formidable Elizabeth does it even better than her mentor and a successful career ensues.

Neil Hornick, London NW11

I have always assumed it was because they have to parade in creations that no normal person would want to be seen dead in. They smile when they receive their pay cheques.

Susan Hora, Reading, Berks

An NHS consultant informed my father that there was a six-month waiting list for his operation, so he paid to see a private consultant (the same man) who operated on him within a week. Would NHS waiting lists be significantly shorter if such queue-jumping was not allowed?

On the contrary. The regulations governing NHS consultants treating private patients specify that they should only do so in addition to their contracted hours of NHS work. It follows that transforming NHS-list patients to the private sector frees time on NHS operating lists, enabling patients originally behind them in the queue to be treated in their stead, thus reducing waiting times down the line.

Bob Heys (retired consultant gynaecologist), Halifax

I am on a twelve-month waiting list at Norfolk & Norwich University NHS Trust hospital for a minor operation to correct a very painful condition. The 'complaints liaison nurse' wrote to me: 'to enable an increase in your priority for surgery this would then be at the expense of other patients who would then have to wait longer (sic).'

Norwich Union Healthcare insurance guarantees prompt treatment and private healthcare benefits at the same hospital – but not for existing conditions! I think this means that the answer to Keith MacDonald's question is no. Or maybe it means yes.

George Sneed, Carleton Rode, Norfolk

If a person were in a coma and needed surgery, would anaesthesia be necessary?

Anaesthesia serves three main functions, each of which can be achieved with a variety of drugs and techniques. Pain relief is used to suppress reflexes such as a fast heart, high blood pressure and limb movements that would occur with a surgical stimulus even if the patient was unconscious and could not feel pain. Muscular relaxation is employed to assist surgical access that is complicated by tense muscles in, say, the abdomen. When these two objectives have been achieved, the patient may be unconscious anyway – many drugs have more than one function. But if not, then unconsciousness may be induced (some operations are carried out awake and this may not be required).

A comatose patient is by definition already unconscious. If they required an operation, then pain relief and relaxation would be used, but anaesthetists would usually include enough 'anaesthetic agent' to be assured of complete unconsciousness as well.

(Dr) Mark Porter, consultant anaesthetist, Burbage, Leics

I once heard that when the first A-bomb was detonated, the scientists actually weren't 100 per cent certain that it wouldn't create a chain reaction throughout the whole atmosphere. Can anyone confirm this?

There is an account of this in Richard Rhodes' *The Making of the Atomic Bomb* (Simon & Schuster), considered by many to be the definitive history of the Manhattan project. The scientists considered it a possibility, but speculated on many things, including the TNT equivalent of the bomb. According to Rhodes, the possibility of setting the atmosphere alight was also considered by the Germans, who were developing a bomb, although with much less enthusiasm and fewer resources.

Philip Clarke, Letchworth, Herts

Yes, it is true. Many of them took the precaution of a substantial life insurance policy.

Ernst van den Doel, Bilthoven, The Netherlands

In the coming weeks, I expect to complete a fully functioning prototype of a perpetual motion machine. If successful, how much money can I expect to make?

If Lou Skannon is successful in making a perpetual motion machine, he will make an infinite amount of money. As there is less money than this in the universe, this might seem to be a problem – but no bigger problem than making a perpetual motion machine in the first place.

Peter Borrows, Amersham Old Town, Bucks

Building a perpetual motion machine is easy – but testing it could take a while.

Dave Garnett, Cambridge

Clearly the answer is 'no end'.

Phil Buglione, London SE21

Nothing. It won't work. (That's a very big 'if' in the question.)

Tim Gossling, Cambridge

Making money from your invention will really depend on your business acumen. I suggest you pass it over to some large manufacturer (after patenting your device of course) that will make your money for you. And if that doesn't work, you will still certainly be awarded the Nobel prize in physics and mathematics, for having disproved more than four hundred years of thinking on the laws of conservation of matter. That will be enough to retire on, I should think.

Malcolm Afferson, Barnsley

Mathematically, you can estimate the expected income by multiplying the money to be made from a working perpetual motion machine by the probability of building one.

A perpetual motion machine means you get something for nothing, so the gains to be made would be vast: let's say £1,000bn a year. However, most scientists would put the probability of building such a machine so close to zero that the expected income comes out to a small fraction of a penny.

The probability is small because a successful perpetual motion machine would falsify either the first or the second law of thermodynamics. This in turn would mean that much of the science and engineering of the past hundred years or so is wrong – an unlikely prospect.

Simon Taylor, Nottingham

When your machine is up and running, you will have overcome the limitations of the law that states that entropy increases with time. The machine itself will be a complete enclosed environment for upholding the law of conservation of energy. In which case, you can use it to travel to any point in the future and discover how rich you are then.

Cliff Lloyd, London NW6

People who invent perpetual motion do not usually make money from their cleverness. Traditionally, they meet with mysterious and fatal accidents. The invention then becomes the sole property of a sinister and enormously powerful American energy conglomerate. Massive corporate muscle is then applied to ensure that the invention produces a history of death and destruction at least as spectacular as its original potential for alleviating suffering and improving the human condition. This is called 'capitalism'.

Mat Curran, Whitley Bay

Will you stop going on and on and on about money!

Peter McPartland, Liverpool

In what order should washing-up be done after a family Sunday roast? And who should do it?

As children, my three brothers and I used to do the Sunday roast dinner washing-up. We did this in two shifts of two people (one of the older two children plus one of the younger two on each shift), supervised/refereed by our father. The washing up was done in order of increasing greasiness – generally pudding cutlery, pudding plates, main course cutlery, main course plates, serving dishes, saucepans and finally the meat tin. We weren't posh enough for a starter.

The first point over which we always argued was what constituted the halfway point. This was generally thought by the first shift to be at the start of the serving dishes, but disputed by the second shift, who thought they should start at the saucepans. The second argument was who had done the second shift last week. If we were very lucky dad would do the meat tin.

We turned this into a race where the drier was deemed to have won if there were fewer than three items in the rack when the washer had finished. I wonder how clean our crockery and cutlery was?

Helen Parkes, Sheffield

There are many ways to order the washing up after a family Sunday roast, but only one sure rule – the person who cooked does none of it.

Elizabeth Atherton, Chester

The scullery maid; crystal first.

Linda Walmsley, Downham, Lancs

This is one of my favourite topics – there is a correct way to wash up after a roast (or any meal). First, get the water as hot as you can stand it, put the cutlery in to soak. Wash and rinse any glasses and cups. Wash the cutlery, then plates in size order. Finally, if the water is clean enough, tackle the saucepans and the roasting tin. This method also means your washing up should be balanced perfectly in the drainer.

As to who does it, when I was a child we always had the dubious honour of washing up after Sunday dinner (hence my sad obsession with how to wash up).

Jane Mitchell-Barnes, Smethwick, Birmingham

What is the highest IQ ever recorded? Does it mean anything?

In the late eighties, the *Guinness Book Of Records* cited an IQ score of 228 achieved by the aptly named Marilyn vos Savant.

IQs used to be calculated by dividing 'mental age', as measured on a standardized test, by actual age and then multiplying by 100. But nowadays it is defined statistically as a normal distribution in which scores are assigned so that 50 per cent of the population score above 100 (the population average), 16 per cent score above 115, 2 per cent score above 130, and so on. This means that about one person in 100 million billion can be expected to score 228 or above. Given the world's population of about five billion, the odds against anyone having such a high IQ are more than 20 million to one.

This suggests that either Ms vos Savant's IQ is meaningless, or she is a walking miracle. If she is a miracle, she must have the intelligence to realize that her IQ is meaningless.

Even if it were credible, it would not be the highest IQ ever recorded. In *Pygmalion Reconsidered* (1971), Elashoff and Snow reveal that Rosenthal and Jacobson, researching the effects of teacher expectations, recorded IQs of 249, 251, 262 and 300 in a single San Francisco primary school. The meaningfulness of IQ scores is debatable but experts agree that no IQ test can be trusted to measure accurately outside the range 60 to 160.

(Dr) Andrew M. Colman, Department of Psychology,
University of Leicester

Are there any valid arguments, other than religious ones, as to why it would be better for the planet for the human race to continue rather than to become extinct?

The questioner asks whether or not it would be better for 'the planet'. This is a problem of values. The planet, in so far as it is a material object, clearly has no values of its own, since values are a product of consciousness. The planet could no more experience pleasure in the continued existence of life than it would lament its passing. It therefore follows that any positive attributes the planet is thought to possess only exist because of their presence in the mind of a living being capable of experiencing them. So far as we know, humans are able to experience more complex and varied responses to the world than any other animal. This opinion may be no more than 'speciesist' vanity, but the existence of anything approaching human levels of creative thought in other animals is so far unproven. In any case, whatever other animals think, we can only answer this question from within our own value system. To this extent it answers itself. The beauties and pleasures of the natural world that we experience are only recognized as such because we are here to do the recognizing. If we didn't exist, neither would these experiences. The planet is only valuable as long as someone is here to value it. Our existence is thus a necessary condition for the continuation of the planet itself as something that is meaningful.

(Dr) P. Barlow, Sunderland University, Tyne and Wear

Dr Barlow's answer is based on the assumption that 'better' necessarily means 'morally superior'; this makes nonsense in the context. In the English language it can also mean 'in a superior physical condition', as when we say that someone is better after an illness. In this sense the planet would obviously be better without the human race. In these days of efficient contraception and when there are few family businesses left to keep going, the main motives for perpetuating the human race must be to satisfy the parental instinct, to attempt to achieve some sort of immortality, or to keep Debrett's Peerage in business. However, it may surprise the questioner to know that two Christian sects, the Albigenses and Cathari in the eleventh to thirteenth centuries in southern France and elsewhere, condemned procreation on the grounds that it increased the amount of evil in the world, which they saw as a battleground between spiritual good and material evil. They were condemned as heretics and became the victims of a crusade led by our Simon de Montfort.

Robert Sephton, Oxford

It was not our Simon de Montfort, Earl of Leicester, born in 1208, who led the merciless crusade against the Albigenses and Cathars in south-west France. It was Simon IV le Fort, Sire de Montfort, who was appointed to lead the crusade in 1209, following the assassination of the papal envoy, Pierre de Castelnau, near St Gilles. Meanwhile, our Simon de Montfort was a babe in arms.

F. Paul Taylor, Frodsham, Cheshire

I wonder if Robert Sephton realizes that by introducing the Albigenses and Cathars into the debate, he undermines his own argument. These sects, like other forms of Manicheism, believed that all matter was evil. For them, the world would be a better place if all biological life were extinguished. By this logic, a healthy planet is a dead planet. So keep up the good work, all you polluters out there!

Flavia Dunford-Trodd, Liverpool

Why is it that to make a cup of tea with milk in the best way, apparently the milk should be put in first?

When tea was first introduced to England in the mid seventeenth century, it was an exclusive and expensive drink, favoured by (and indeed only afforded by) the upper classes. Later, the whole paraphernalia of afternoon tea with cakes became fashionable for those who had the leisure time and money to afford it.

The pottery industry responded to the elitist nature of tea drinking by creating delicate, expensive china. The finest china was considered too fragile to withstand the scalding hot tea, so the milk was poured in first to cool the temperature. As tea became more affordable to all sections of society it still retained its genteel image, and it became a mark of class and sophistication to suggest that the china would crack if the tea were poured in first.

Therefore, although most of us now drink our tea from mugs, the custom of putting the milk in first is a throwback to historical elitism.

Catherine Black, Tachbrook, Warks

When cold milk is mixed with hot tea, its temperature is raised. When this happens, chemical changes occur in some of the constituents of the milk. The precise nature of these changes, and hence of the new compounds formed, varies according to the speed at which the temperature rises. When the tea is poured into the milk, there is, in the initial stages of pouring, only a small amount of hot tea in cold milk, and hence the temperature of the milk rises comparatively slowly. When the milk is poured into the tea, there is a small amount of cold milk in a large amount of hot tea and the temperature of the milk rises very quickly.

The different chemicals produced by the different rates of temperature rise have different tastes. Most people seem to prefer the taste of those produced by the slower rate of warming.

George Kitchin, Tirril, Penrith

Milk is an emulsion. There are tiny drops of fat that are evenly distributed in a watery medium. The drops are so small that they don't coalesce into a big fatty mass until the milk goes sour through bacterial action. If the milk is put into the cup before the tea is poured the milk is diluted and heated slowly and the emulsion remains intact, but if the milk is added to a hot liquid and diluted quickly some of the emulsion breaks down and you tend to get droplets of oil on the surface of the tea.

Why the upper classes insist on adding milk last I can't guess, but what do they know?

Paul Diamond, Woodford Green, Essex

Nick Arnold's Horrible Science book *Chemical Chaos* gives the following description:

> Milk contains a chemical called casein (cay-sin). When tea mixes with milk its chemicals break down the casein into smaller molecules. If you add the milk to the tea it means that more casein gets broken down. This makes the tea taste of boiled milk. That's why chemists in the know add tea to milk and not the other way around!

Angus Holford, London E12

Whether you put milk into the cup before or after the tea has nothing to do with the taste of the drink and everything to do with social class. I once heard an upper-middle-class lady describe an acquaintance who didn't quite make the grade as, 'A bit, well, MIF, you know'.

Gerald Haigh, Bedworth, Warks

My Auntie Sally, who kept a boarding house in Scarborough in the forties, ordered all her guests to 'Put t'milk in first or y'll crack me cups.' Hence 'milk in first' can be associated with the lower classes and cheap crockery.

My own preference is to put the milk in last, for you can't really tell how much milk to put in until you can gauge the strength of the tea. In my experience, the 'milk in first' brigade usually put in too much milk and produce an insipid and unrefreshing drink.

Peter Wrigley, Birstall, Yorks

Oh, no, no, no. Pouring hot water straight on to the bag or leaves encourages a full and fast diffusion of the tea, and milk can be added afterwards, which also gives you the benefit of being able to judge when the perfect shade of beige appears (at which point one stops pouring the milk).

When tea-making occurs in a pot, the milk is added to the cup first, in impatient anticipation of the full brewing (especially when my father makes tea in a pot for five people, and refuses to use more than one tea bag!).

Celia Davis, Cornwall

The question may not have a scientific answer, but it is a poser that is very well known to students of statistics.

In the twenties, R. A. Fisher, the founder of modern statistical methods, devised an experiment to test the assertion by a colleague that she could always tell the difference. Eight cups of tea were prepared, into four of which the milk was poured first. In the remaining four, the milk was added later. The cups were presented to the lady in random order. He then calculated the probability that the number of correct guesses could be the result of pure chance, rather than skill on the part of the subject.

This experiment is described in detail in his pioneering book *Statistical Methods for Research Workers*, and the circumstances are recorded in his daughter's biography, *R. A. Fisher, The Life of a Scientist* by Joan Fisher Box.

Gavin Ross, Harpenden, Herts

George Orwell, the Old Etonian and upper-middle-lower-class novelist, made a very good case for milk last in his essay, 'A Nice Cup Of Tea':

The milk-first school can bring forward some fairly strong arguments, but I maintain that my own argument is unanswerable. This is that, by putting the tea in first and stirring as one pours, one can exactly regulate the amount of milk whereas one is liable to put in too much milk if one does it the other way round.

Jon Mackintosh, Winchester, Hants

It's reassuring to read affirmation that my personal pouring practice, adding milk to tea, distinguishes one from *hoi polloi*. Just to make sure I'm getting it absolutely right, though: is it posher to take the teabag out of the mug before or after adding the milk?

Tim Kingston, Luton

Nobody seems to have mentioned, so far, a possible practical reason for putting milk in the cup first. For those not using the refinement of a tea strainer and making tea from leaf tea, milk put in first seems to keep the tea leaves at the bottom of the cup, whereas if put in last, they tend to float.

Berry Kenny, Elsworth, Cambs

Not strictly relevant, but there was a competition a while back to find the worst-made tea. First prize was deservedly awarded to the British engineering firm where, each Monday, the teaboy was sent to buy a packet of loose tea, a bag of sugar and a tin of condensed milk. These were mixed together and rolled out into as many little balls as there were tea breaks in the week. Each tea break, one ball was put in a jug which was then filled from the hot tap in the gents.

John Coatman, Sheffield

The Wadham College Tea Society has discussed this issue

at some length without reaching any firm conclusions. One contingent of our membership swears by the pouring of the milk last, claiming that it allows the tea drinker to gauge the correct amount of milk needed for the given cup.

However, a dissenting faction of 'Milk-firsters' argues that if one claims to know how to make a decent cup of tea, one should already be aware of how much milk to pour in. And anyway, it's just proper that way.

Overall, we have made it society policy to welcome tea drinkers whatever their preference, and recommend that the tea drinking public at large do the same. May we all unite under the banner of Libertea, Fraternitea and Egalitea.

> *Tim Partridge and Paul O'Connor, on behalf of*
> *Wadham Tea Soc, Oxford University*

What is the oldest trick in the book?

Send me £200 and I'll tell you.

> *Stuart McLagan, Dundee, Scotland*

Saying to the electorate (in effect): 'I may have been rubbish for the past few years, but I promise I'll mend my ways if you vote me in again.'

> *Richard Cooper, Twickenham*

At school in the forties I cannot remember any fellow pupils being hyperactive, disruptive or showing symptoms similar to attention deficit hyperactivity disorder. Is the recent growth of this due to a lack of firm discipline at home and in school, or to pollution, radiation, junk food, etc.?

There are always fashions in mental illnesses. In Freud's day conversion hysteria was popular. Now it is rarely found. In Sydney, where I was working as an educational psychologist, any child with a behavioural or learning difficulty was likely to be diagnosed as autistic. Since then, this diagnosis has come to be used much more discriminatingly.

Nowadays the psychiatric profession, supported by the drug companies, readily creates fashions in diagnosis. The committee that decides upon the contents of *The Diagnostic and Statistical Manual* (DSM) of the American Psychiatric Association, a manual that is increasingly used here, needs only ascertain that a group of psychiatrists reliably agree that a mental disorder exists in order to include this disorder in the manual. Another committee could reliably agree that the moon was made of green cheese, but such agreement does not prove the cheesiness of the moon.

There have always been children who do not behave in

the ways in which the adults around them wish. A few of these children have some actual brain dysfunction. Many more children, living under conditions that they find stressful, are constantly distracted by anxiety and so are hyperactive and disruptive. Other children have parents and teachers who cannot tolerate the exuberant behaviour of ordinary children and wish them to become unremittingly quiet and obedient. The current popularity of the recently created mental disorder ADHD means that many anxious or ordinary children are diagnosed as ADHD and prescribed Ritalin or similar potentially addictive drugs. Their long-term effects on a developing brain are yet to be discovered.

Dorothy Rowe, London N5

Why are teeth thought worthy of a separate medical profession, when all other parts of the body are looked after by specialist doctors?

Apart from dentists, there are other 'paramedical' professions, e.g. clinical psychologists (as distinct from psychiatrists, who are medical specialists), child psychotherapists and chiropodists. In the US and the Netherlands, dentists must take a full medical degree. If this is wasteful, so must be our requirement of, say, eye surgeons or psychiatrists so to do. There is then a need for an abbreviated medical curriculum, restricted to the shared needs of all specialists.

Richard Benjamin, London N11

Having worked in many doctors' mouths, I am convinced they have little personal understanding of this part of their own body.

Tim Cudmore, Windhoek, Namibia

We often hear people described as 'intellectuals'. I would like to be one. Can this be achieved by reading selected books? If so, which?

The main requirement not only for being an 'intellectual', but being a wise one, is to be well-grounded in philosophy, though few people lauded as such fulfil this criterion. Aristotle's advice is to start with what's best understood. Two of today's clearest, most reader-friendly introductions are Donald Palmer's *Does The Centre Hold: An Introduction To Western Philosophy* (Mayfield, 1996) and Brian Fay's *Contemporary Philosophy Of Social Science: A Multicultural Approach* (Blackwell, 1966).

Books, though, aren't enough. Philosophy requires discussion in classes between teachers and students, and clarifying your thoughts through putting them down in writing and/or pictures.

David Rodway (lecturer in art and philosophy), Kensington &
Chelsea College, London SW10

The qualifications for recognition as an intellectual vary from country to country. As a rough guide: in Germany, someone who has written a book about Hegel; in America, someone who has read Hegel; in England, someone who has heard of Hegel.

Peter Yearwood, Reading

To be an intellectual is to possess the qualities of understanding and reasoning, and to be able to see all sides of an argument. It is not necessary to read selected books, although learning is always useful. The poet John Donne put it more eloquently: 'On a huge hill, Craiged and steep, Truth stands, and hee that will Reach her, about must, and about must goe.'

(Mrs) Pat James, Bristol

One book might suffice: *An Incomplete Education*, by Judy Jones and William Wilson (Unwin Hyman), in which two New York writers give a functionally literate dilettante enough lines to impress fellow pseuds. For example, the whole of the Shakespeare lexicon is covered in seventeen pages and summed up in D. H. Lawrence's 'When I read Shakespeare I am struck with wonder/That such trivial people should muse and thunder/In such lovely language.'

Nigel Clarke, Perth, Western Australia

At Christmas dinner with my parents, I made reference to the *Guardian*. Conversation halted. The silence was broken by my mother: 'Oh,' she said, ' . . . an intellectual.' My parents are *Daily Telegraph* readers.

Cicely Heaviside, Huddersfield

Could there be a more generally fascinating and frivolous job than a Notes & Queries editor?

Four words here: Fascinating, Frivolous, Job and Editor. Put the first and the third together and you have what the fourth does sorting out the second.

Hedley McConnell, Tenerife, Spain